"Matthew Bates calls the church to recove a gospel which is beautiful, bountiful, and transformative. Bates masterfully shows how the fully orbed gospel of the biblical witness is still good news for 'nones' and 'dones,' those without religion, and those who have walked away from it. An ideal book for Bible study groups who want to be reminded of why the gospel is indeed 'good news.'"

—**Michael F. Bird**
academic dean and lecturer in New Testament,
Ridley College

"In *Why the Gospel?*, Matthew Bates seeks to demonstrate that the kingship of Christ is central to the gospel and is the reason for the gospel. While one may not agree with all of the moves Bates makes, the underlying aim of the book is apropos for this historic moment in the church—it challenges the reader to think again about what the gospel is and why the gospel matters for our time. A provocative read."

—**Lisa Bowens**
associate professor of New Testament,
Princeton Theological Seminary

"Matthew Bates expertly uses Scripture to refurbish the gospel. But he doesn't park the gospel along a scholarly roadside, he insists: God intends restorative action—Let's drive! Bates invites readers on a journey of knowing the king who is the good news."

—**Nijay Gupta**
professor of New Testament, Northern Seminary

"I recommend this book because it will challenge the reader to develop his or her own practical discipleship theology. To sustain disciple-making movements, we need biblical substance. Bates asks us to examine Scripture to discover why King Jesus is rescuing us. In learning why, we find ourselves able to better live and share the gospel purposefully today. Read and wrestle with this book; I am very glad that I did."

—**Bobby Harrington**
pastor and CEO of discipleship.org and renew.org

"Previous generations asked if there was evidence to support the claims of Christianity. Mountains of apologetic resources were created to address this question. But a new generation has emerged that isn't focused on the gospel's credibility, but rather its plausibility. Before asking whether it's true they want to know why the gospel even matters. Matthew Bates has written the book our generation needs. He not only helps us rediscover the radical message of Jesus and his apostles, but he shows why this gospel is far larger than a narrow call to individual salvation. It's the message the church, and the world, has been waiting for."

—Skye Jethani
author and cohost of *The Holy Post* podcast

"A provocative book because the church needs this kind of provocation, *Why the Gospel?* draws from complex and cutting-edge research to present timeless truths with inviting clarity. Anyone who senses that the gospel they've received is a tepid and ineffective counterfeit to God's revelation of grace and power will benefit from Bates's bold reminder that Jesus is King."

—Amy Peeler
associate professor of New Testament, Wheaton College

"Bates reminds us that the core of the gospel concerns Jesus's kingship. This helps reorient the why of gospel. Too often we narrow the message of Christianity and forget that the gospel is about all of life, not merely inward renewal. While we can describe the gospel in a variety of ways, this book rightly gives us the cosmic picture of what God is doing in this world."

—Patrick Schreiner
associate professor of New Testament,
Midwestern Baptist Theological Seminary;
author of *The Ascension of Christ*

Why the Gospel?

Living the Good News
of King Jesus with Purpose

Matthew W. Bates

WILLIAM B. EERDMANS PUBLISHING COMPANY
GRAND RAPIDS, MICHIGAN

Wm. B. Eerdmans Publishing Co.
4035 Park East Court SE, Grand Rapids, Michigan 49546
www.eerdmans.com

Book design by Leah Luyk

Printed in the United States of America

29 28 27 26 25 24   2 3 4 5 6 7

ISBN 978-0-8028-8168-7

Library of Congress Cataloging-in-Publication Data

A catalog record for this book is available from the Library of Congress.

Scripture quotations labeled NIV are from the New International Version. Scripture quotations labeled AT are the author's own translation.

For my sister, Katie Erickson.
With gratitude for your energetic support, prayers, and enthusiasm
. . . and with much love.

CONTENTS

FOREWORD

This powerful new study of the gospel by Matthew Bates takes us where we have not gone often enough, to the *why* of the gospel. Yet for the sake of the church's health and mission today, this is exactly where we need to go. We need to journey into the gospel's *purposes*. Bates's book points out a fresh path, then expertly guides us down it.

Why is urgent because the gospel that many accepted, many believe, many preach and teach, and that many have inscribed into official church statements is deconstructing the church. I have elsewhere described this gospel as "soterian" because it is narrowly concerned with the salvation associated with personal forgiveness. Folks may no longer be coming to church in their Sunday finest, but many are sitting in pews every Sunday, all too comfortable, because they are confident that the gospel means they are "saved" or "justified" or "going to heaven when they die."

This all-too-comfortable feeling stems from a deficient understanding of the gospel in the Bible. Yet millions have accepted such ideas as the full gospel truth and enshrined them in gospel tracts, gospel sermons, and evangelistic methods. They have been further institutionalized by worship services that speak about the saving benefits of Jesus's death but little else. But a gospel that foregrounds personal forgiveness is *not* the gospel of Jesus, not the gospel of Peter, not the gospel of Paul, and it is not the gospel of anyone else in the New Testament.

This is why Matthew Bates's study of the gospel's *why* is pressing for the church and practical. Bates has a wonderful section in this book on various "malformed gospels." Beyond that, his chapters will generate a thousand conversations, as he unlocks what Scripture says about the gospel's *why* in an innovative yet faithful fashion. He discusses the cycle of glory, holistic restoration, personal transformation, why "nones" are disinterested in Christianity and how to engage them, and many other topics.

Since the storyline about the gospel's *why* is captivating, and I don't want to reveal too much, I'll leave you to read what Bates has to say for yourself. But to provide a frame, let's back up and discuss why the gospel in Scripture is about more than personal salvation. The gospel of Jesus in the Gospels is about the *kingdom of God*, not first and foremost about your sins or my sins, but about how God's kingdom is arriving through Jesus's kingship. There are four Gospels but one message. That message is *the gospel*, which is why we call them "Gospels."

Over and over in the Gospels the reader is summoned to answer one simple question: Who is this man? The primary question is not, How can I get saved? Nor is it, How can I go to heaven when I die? No, over and over the question is about the identity of Jesus.

That Jesus's identity is a gospel matter is apparent in how each Gospel begins. Take the Gospel of Matthew's opening genealogy: it leads us name by name to "Jesus who is called the Messiah" (1:17, NIV), and it's done. Next, consider Mark's first verse: "The beginning of the good news about Jesus the Messiah, the Son of God" (1:1, NIV). Mark effectively starts with the end. He states his conclusion at the opening in order to teach the reader how to interpret the whole: the gospel is about Jesus, and he is the royal Son of God. Third, notice how Luke presents an orderly narrative of "things that have been fulfilled among us" (1:1, NIV), but it is about Jesus or points to him over and over. Finally, there's John, and you can't get more Jesus-centered than this: "In the beginning was the Word, and the Word was with God, and the Word was God" (1:1, NIV).

Beyond its opening, the famous "I Am" sayings of John's Gospel are pure gospel announcements, invitations, and articulations. Jesus *Is*; therefore the gospel *is* announced.

The content of the message in the Gospels is that the kingdom of God has drawn near because Jesus is the king. The gospel's primary purpose follows from that: we need to know who the king is and to become allegiant to him. As the installed king, King Jesus saves and rescues and justifies and sanctifies and glorifies. Those acts don't make him the king. Those acts are because he is the king. Bates is right: first king.

Bates and I—and we stand alongside N. T. Wright and other like-minded scholars—have no desire to push redemption or forgiveness into a corner of the room, so that kingship can take its place in the center. Our contention has always been a *both–and*. That is, *both* Yes to kingship *and* Yes to forgiveness. But the order matters. If we are careless about the order, then King Jesus becomes a tool for some other end rather than the essence of the gospel. We preach, as Paul himself says it, "The Christ crucified" or "The King crucified." Jesus is not a lackey, but the cosmic Lord who has generously given himself so that we can receive benefits.

We want to be equipped to live and share the good news. If the gospel is that Jesus is the King, then discipleship is about allegiance to King Jesus. Matthew Bates's *Why the Gospel?* will help you discover God's fullest gospel purposes, so that you and others can more thoroughly embrace a lifestyle of loyal discipleship.

Scot McKnight
Professor of New Testament
Northern Seminary

Introduction

Not *what* but *why*. The questions we ask determine what we see.
Numerous books ask, *What is the gospel?* Rightly so. The gospel
is the greatest gift God could ever give us. Praise God for his generous rescue! Moreover, it is urgent that we hold fast to the gospel
we find in the Bible.

I remain passionate that the church safeguard and share the true
gospel. I've contributed to this *what-is-the-gospel* effort through previous books, especially *Gospel Allegiance* and *The Gospel Precisely*.
These books, and others like them, primarily describe the gospel's
saving message, its content.

But this book is unique. It is unique not because everyone is
ignoring what Scripture teaches about the gospel—although sadly
many are—but because it allows fresh answers to emerge by asking
new questions. Countless books ask what the gospel is. But to the
best of my knowledge, no book on the gospel has ever been written
that fronts what may prove to be an even more important question:
Why the gospel?

If we want to know God's heart, then the gospel's *why* is even
more vital than its *what,* because it carefully attends to God's motives. God has given us the gospel. But for what ultimate purposes
and final reasons? And what intermediate steps is God using to bring
about those final aims? If we want a deep relationship with God, we
need to know not just the what of the gospel, but also the why.

1

Why the Gospel? also suggests a different but related set of questions that this book will touch on. Granted the smorgasbord of lifestyle options available in today's world, why should anyone respond to this bizarre cross-and-resurrection story? And when a person does respond, but discovers that journeying with Jesus truly involves self-death, why continue to cling to this purportedly "good news"? In other words, why is the gospel still compelling in the contemporary world? These additional questions are especially pertinent to mission and evangelism—although discerning Christians recognize that the church itself is part of the mission field. We *all* need to be won over by Jesus again and again.

Even if you've never thought to ask these questions, doubtless you already have preliminary ideas regarding why God gave the gospel and why it remains attractive. But how well do your ideas align with what the Bible emphasizes in its full counsel? As I've taught about salvation over the years, I've found that the answers most often advanced about the *why* of the gospel are either flat-out wrong from a biblical standpoint, or they are partially right but disconnected from what Scripture says about the gospel's widest purposes and ultimate aims.

This book is designed to complement studies that emphasize the gospel's content by offering a novel exploration of a different but related issue: the gospel's purpose. It is written for a general audience—anyone!—but it has been specially crafted for church-wide studies, small groups, Christian classes, pastors, and church leaders. Questions at the end of each chapter can facilitate group conversation or individual reflection.

Can I ask a favor? If you find this book helpful, please spread the word. Share what you're learning with others by applying its ideas in conversation. Mention it on social media. Use it for discussion groups. Give it a positive star rating or review on a bookseller's website. Such things help a book succeed in today's publishing world. However you opt to help, please do it in a way that elevates King Jesus.

We want to live gospel-centered lives in our churches and families, and as individuals. We ache for the brokenness to be mended. We want money-grubbers to become sacrificial givers, sex addicts to learn to be faithful, ladder climbers to grow into servant leaders. We ache because we are complicit in the brokenness ourselves. But we have begun to experience mending. We know the gospel is the source of healing for ourselves and for our hurting world. So we rejoice! The gospel is indeed the best possible news.

But it is undeniable that there is much confusion about the gospel in the church. This book is about the gospel's purpose—or better, how the gospel's primary purpose relates to its many purposes. Confusion is alleviated when we explore the gospel's aims. And we gain even more.

Attention to the why of the gospel also helps us see its content more clearly. Knowing why positions us to respond to the gospel in the fullest possible way ourselves. It also prepares us, so we can tell the good news to others in a true and effective manner. In other words, when as we answer *Why the gospel?* we also gain fresh insights into related questions: *What is the gospel?* and *How should we live out the gospel today?* and *How can I share the gospel well with others?*

My greatest hope for this book is that it will cause a Jesus-is-king revolution, causing more and more people to recover their divinely intended glory so that they can fully honor the one true God.

QUESTIONS FOR DISCUSSION OR REFLECTION

1. Describe some of your first memories of hearing the gospel. Who shared it? What was emphasized?
2. What is the gospel? How would you demonstrate from Scripture that your description of the gospel is correct? (Although

this book focuses on the *why* of the gospel, if you are eager to see how it summarizes the *what*, you can sneak a peek at chapter 4).

3. What are some of your preliminary ideas about why God gave the gospel?
4. What do you think motivates people to respond to the gospel today?
5. What is your own story with regard to gospel response? Think past and present.

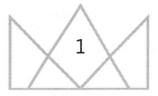

King First

I was not deliberately disobeying God. Don't misunderstand; I've done that more times than I'd care to admit. But not this time. I was making the best choice under the circumstances—at least so I thought.

Yes, I was a self-absorbed twenty-five-year-old. But I was making an effort to hear God's voice. Yet deep down, where heart is set aflame by the Spirit, I knew my choice wasn't right. I needed what only the gospel could give. But because I'd misunderstood the shape and purpose of the gospel, I didn't know that at the time.

Eighteen months prior, my wife and I had left for Canada with high hopes and plenty of money to pay for schooling. I was pursuing a master's degree in biblical studies at Regent College in Vancouver. But I had invested the money in tech stocks. During my first year at Regent, the only thing dropping faster than the stock market was the pit of my stomach. Would we have enough? Could I even finish school?

The degree not fully completed, we ran out of money and had to leave Canada. We put our U-Haul on a credit card because we didn't even have enough cash to move back to the United States. Knowing that I could at least find forestry work and enjoy family, we headed to my hometown in Northern California.

But God had given me a dream; my life had been transformed as an undergraduate. I was studying physics and engineering when a course on the New Testament flipped my world. After that, I knew I was called to teach Scripture so I could help others experience Jesus. Teaching the Bible was my vocation, something I would always do, even if it never provided a paycheck.

Now that I was back in my hometown, I struggled over what I should do with my life. Forestry work paid the bills but didn't make my heart sing. It could never be more than a stopgap. Should I return to engineering? Something else? I needed direction. I pleaded with God, urgently.

Then I made a series of mistakes. As you'll hear, God was gracious nevertheless. But if I had more fully grasped the gospel, I could have better served others and avoided much personal hassle.

Simply a King

At that stage of my life I was only just beginning to grasp the gospel. Or better, the gospel was just beginning to grip me. In Christian circles we speak about the gospel so frequently yet so vaguely that what should be clear has become murky.

Why did God give us the gospel? Popular Christian culture and much academic theology urge us to think we receive *something else* first in the gospel. Soon we'll explore why putting something else first has had a devastating effect on our churches and evangelistic efforts.

What that *something else* might be varies among Christian groups, but one answer is most common. A couple months ago I was teaching a group of pastors. At the time I was beginning to draft this book, so as a test I decided to ask them: Why the gospel? Predictably they gave the answer I most often see and hear: "forgiveness of sins." On the one hand, this is a fine answer, since forgiveness of sins is frequently mentioned in Scripture as a purpose or intended outcome when the gospel is proclaimed (for example, 1 Cor. 15:3; Acts 2:38; 5:31; 10:43). So this answer is partially correct. But on

6

the other hand, as we'll see, forgiveness is not the most accurate starting point.

So after affirming the group's basic sensibilities, I pressed them: "But why do we need to be forgiven?" It is nearly impossible to get a room full of pastors to stop talking, but when I asked this, they fell silent. They had taken it for granted that the main aim of the gospel is forgiveness for forgiveness' sake, so they were rendered speechless.

Ten years ago, when I would ask questions about the gospel's main purpose, church leaders would inevitably say, "So we can go to heaven." But it is increasingly well known that the Bible never directly says the purpose is heaven. This group of pastors was savvy enough to avoid saying that the gospel or forgiveness is purposed primarily toward getting a person into heaven, but they were uncertain what a better answer might be.

Why the uncertainty?

Because we are convinced that we receive *something else* first in the gospel.

What is that *something else*? Beyond forgiveness of sins for heaven, I've heard other suggestions: a new heart, new birth, justification, righteousness, holiness, regeneration, new life, to be with God forever, escape from hell. Yet none of this is what Scripture tells us.

I have also heard "to be with Jesus" as the answer. Closer, but not exactly. The purpose of the gospel is to connect us to Jesus. But we must ask: Jesus in what capacity?

Never once in teaching this material to groups has someone immediately given Scripture's clearest answer. From a biblical standpoint, why did God give us the gospel?

A king.

God gave the gospel first of all because we need a king.

The gospel is king first. When the Bible describes the proclamation of the good news, again and again the summarizing message is simply that Jesus is the Christ.

Every day in the temple and from house to house, they did not cease teaching and gospeling, "The Christ is Jesus." (Acts 5:42, AT)

Now those who were scattered went about gospeling the word. Philip went down to the city of Samaria and proclaimed to them the Christ. (Acts 8:4–5, AT)

Yet Saul . . . baffled the Jews living in Damascus by proving that Jesus is the Christ. (Acts 9:22, AT)

Paul . . . reasoned with them from the Scriptures, explaining and proving that it was necessary for the Christ to suffer and to rise from the dead, and saying, "This is the Christ, this Jesus, whom I am proclaiming to you." (Acts 17:2–3, AT)

Paul was occupied by preaching, testifying to the Jews that Jesus is the Messiah. (Acts 18:5, AT)

According to Scripture, the gospel is not best captured by saying that Jesus is my Savior, the source of my regeneration, my righteousness, my atoning sacrifice, or my forgiveness. He is those things. But! The gospel is best summarized as *Jesus is the Christ*. And we dare not suggest that what God gave as the essence of the gospel was aimless or irrelevant. That means, if the gospel is primarily that God has given us a *Christ*, then he must have had excellent reasons.

If we want to know God's saving purposes and his heart in giving the gospel, it is incumbent to begin by asking: *Why a messiah?*

First and foremost, the good news is this: *God has given us a king.* When we better understand what "messiah" means, and how the messianic hope developed, we discover that we do not need something else first. A king is exactly what we need.

Why "Christ" Determines Gospel Purpose

When the New Testament claims that Jesus is the Christ or the Messiah, this does not suggest in and of itself that he saves people from their personal sins. Ultimately he does do that. But we must not miss the main point: good news! We have a new king!

But the way our translations of the Bible, songs, and theology textbooks speak about Jesus obscures how the gospel is a royal proclamation. When we are more thoughtful about how we refer to Jesus in our practices, we begin to recover the royal purpose of the gospel in our daily lives.

Calling Jesus the Christ: Then

Jesus Christ is *a claim not a name*. That is, we should *never* think Jesus Christ is simply his name. It is a claim, an assertion about Jesus's identity. Jesus Christ means Jesus is the Christ. When we sing a song with lyrics such as, "Christ alone, cornerstone," we should never think "Christ" means the same thing as "Jesus." It doesn't.

Our New Testament authors are not shy about referring to Jesus as the Christ. The New Testament refers to "Jesus [the] Christ" 135 times. Meanwhile, the apostle Paul uses the alternative "[the] Christ, Jesus" 89 more times. This claim is the essence of the good news. For example, the first thing we learn about Jesus in Mark, the first Gospel that was written, is that the gospel pertains to Jesus as messiah: "The gospel of Jesus Christ" (1:1). To call Jesus of Nazareth instead Jesus *Christ* is to assert that he is a specific type of king. Jesus Christ is a claim that Jesus is the Messiah, not a name.

Analogies can help us understand the significance of Jesus *Christ*. Consider George Washington. There are diverse ways that you could accurately refer to him: The first president of the United States of America; President Washington; General Washington. Or you could just call him by his first name, George. During his lifetime, he also accrued unofficial honorific titles. He was called "The Father of His Country" and "His Excellency." But it would introduce dreadful confusion if we were mistakenly to think the name George Washington means the same thing as "His Excellency," or that they

> *Jesus Christ is a claim that Jesus is the Messiah, not a name.*

are interchangeable. When we say, "George Washington, *His Excellency*," we are combining his name with a reverential title that honors his social stature as head of state. Jesus *Christ* is similar.

If we want to be more exacting, we can look at analogies from Jesus's own time. Matthew Novenson, in his book *Christ Among the Messiahs*, points out examples. A warrior named Judas, son of Mattathias of Modein, came to be called Judas Maccabee. Maccabee was not his name but means "the hammerer." Calling him Judas *Maccabee* combined his name with a reverential title to celebrate his military might.

Or consider the Roman emperor who was reigning when Jesus was born. His name was Octavian. But Octavian was honored by the Roman Senate in 27 BC when he was declared "augustus," that is, exalted or venerable. This title came to be so closely associated with Octavian that today he is frequently called *Caesar Augustus*. When Octavian is called *Caesar Augustus*, a claim is being advanced regarding his venerable stature.

Originally it was much the same when Jesus was called instead Jesus *Christ*. It is accurate to call him Jesus of Nazareth or Jesus son of Joseph (legal) or Jesus son of Mary (actual). But these titles do not reverence him. By calling him Jesus *Christ*, our New Testament authors were claiming that God honored him with the ultimate kingship. God has exalted Jesus to his right hand where he reigns as the Messiah.

Calling Jesus the Christ: Now

We should cease treating Jesus and Christ as if they are interchangeable words. Let's aim to be intentional and precise in how we refer to him. Here are four suggestions for how we can better speak about Jesus as our gospel hope today. First, because the meaning of Christ is not readily apparent to the average person, but king is, call him instead *King Jesus*. Calling him King Jesus is a way to preach the gospel every time you refer to him.

Alternatively, try *Messiah Jesus* or *Jesus the Messiah*. Since many people recognize "messiah" as an ultimate rescuer or leader announced in the Old Testament (the Hebrew Bible), it helps folks better discern Jesus's significance as part of God's wider purposes for the world through Israel as God's chosen people.

Third, instead of Jesus Christ, say *Jesus the Christ*. It doesn't mean anything different than Jesus Christ. In fact, it is a shame that English translations of the Bible don't opt for it. But it is disruptive. It forces listeners to linger over Jesus's office and title.

Fourth, when fitting, take others deeper. Our efforts to emphasize Jesus's kingship are strengthened when we can explain how "Christ" became a reverential title. Consider this next section a guide to the most important information. Draw from it to fill out your own understanding in preparation for sharing the good news with others.

Hope for a Messiah-King

First, what does *Christ* or *Messiah* mean? *Anointed one.* Do you recall how Samuel indicated that David had been chosen as God's new king? Seven sons were passed by, but when David was brought forward, Samuel poured oil on his head (1 Sam. 16:11–13). The anointing with oil set him apart.

In Hebrew the term for anointing is *mashach*. Meanwhile a person who is anointed is a *meshiach*, from which we derive messiah.

It is much the same in the New Testament. The Greek word for anointing is *chriō* and an anointed person is a *christos*; hence the title *Christ*.

In the Old Testament, certain individuals were anointed with oil in order to be set apart for special service to God. This included priests, kings, and prophets (Exod. 40:13; 2 Sam. 2:4; 1 Kings 1:34; 19:16). Yet as we shall see, in the Old Testament time period *the messiah* came to be specially associated with a coming king.

God's Promise to David

God speaks of humans ruling from the beginning. Humans are made in God's image in order to rule creation on God's behalf. But humans opted to decide for themselves what is good and evil. In so doing they rejected God's rule over themselves—and by extension rejected God's rule through them over creation. Since it is crucial to the gospel's purpose in Scripture, we will explore this further in subsequent chapters. For our present purposes, we can leap ahead to subsequent developments in God's relationship with his people.

God's covenants with his people forcefully shaped the boundaries of his future rule. Specifically, God promised to bless all nations on earth through Abraham's offspring (Gen. 12:3; 18:18; 22:18). Then, much later, God echoed the promise to Abraham through a more specific promise to King David:

> When your days are over and you rest with your ancestors, I will raise up your offspring to succeed you, your own flesh and blood, and I will establish his kingdom. He is the one who will build a house for my Name, and I will establish the throne of his kingdom forever. I will be his father, and he will be my son. . . . Your house and your kingdom will endure forever before me; your throne will be established forever. (2 Sam. 7:12–16, NIV)

Notice that God promised to give this offspring of David something quite specific. It is not a vague promise that God will work through David's line. Rather, the Davidic kingdom will endure forever through the establishment of an *eternal throne*.

This promise of the establishment of an eternal throne for David's offspring was celebrated in various psalms:

> You said, "I have made a covenant with my chosen one, I have sworn to David my servant, 'I will establish your line forever and make your throne firm through all generations.'" (Ps. 89:3–4, NIV; see also 89:20, 27–29)

> The LORD swore an oath to David, a sure oath he will not revoke: "One of your own descendants I will place on your throne." (Ps. 132:11, NIV)

As part of God's plan to restore humans so they can rule creation for him, God made outstanding promises to David. God indicated that David's offspring would possess an everlasting throne.

The Failure of God's Promise?

But then God's promise failed—or so it seemed. First the Assyrians conquered and scattered Israel in 722 BC. Then the Babylonians defeated Judah in 586 BC, leveling the temple and taking captives. Afterward there was no Davidic king on the throne. Only the faintest glimmer of hope was present: at least the rightful Davidic king, Jehoiachin, was still alive. But he was in Babylon, no longer ruling (2 Kings 25:27–30).

Eventually some of the Judean captives returned from exile to reinhabit the promised land, but no Davidic kingship emerged. Instead the Judeans were governed by foreign powers and a local high priest. Independence was briefly regained after the success of the Maccabean revolt (164 BC), but a Davidic dynasty never took root.

God's Renewed Promises

Yet God's promises do not fail. He says, "My word that goes out from my mouth: It will not return to me empty, but will accomplish what I desire and achieve the purpose for which I sent it" (Isa. 55:11, NIV). In these dark seasons of scattering and exile, God sent multiple prophets to announce that the previous Davidic promises were not botched prophecies. Instead, speaking on God's behalf, the prophets doubled down on God's infinite trustworthiness.

In the midst of bleak circumstances, God announced that his promises to David of an eternal throne for his family would be fulfilled in the future:

> For to us a child is born, to us a son is given, and the government will be on his shoulders. And he will be called Wonderful Counselor, Mighty God, Everlasting Father, Prince of Peace. Of the greatness of his government and peace there will be no end. He will reign on David's throne and over his kingdom, establishing and upholding it with justice and righteousness from that time on and forever. The zeal of the LORD Almighty will accomplish this. (Isa. 9:6–7, NIV)

> "The days are coming," declares the LORD, "when I will raise up for David a righteous Branch, a King who will reign wisely and do what is just and right in the land. In his days Judah will be saved and Israel will live in safety. This is the name by which he will be called: The LORD Our Righteous Savior." (Jer. 23:5–6, NIV; see also 33:14–16)

> My servant David will be king over them, and they will all have one shepherd. They will follow my laws and be careful to keep my

decrees. They will live in the land I gave to my servant Jacob, the land where your ancestors lived. They and their children and their children's children will live there forever, and David my servant will be their prince forever. (Ezek. 37:24–25, NIV)

Through such prophecies, God affirmed not only that he would keep his promise to David, but more. There would be a future king. O, but what a king!

The Incomparable Coming King

God's prophets announced that the messiah's reign would be marvelous—bringing justice, peace, safety, prosperity, and blessings. In short, the messiah's reign and governance would be incomparable. In fact, the messiah's reign would have universal significance, reaching outsiders too—the gentile nations. The messiah would be a Jewish king of such tremendous international stature that his rule would ultimately benefit the nations.

Diverse Messianic Hopes

As the first century AD dawned, the expectation of a future king was palpable but fluid. For example, those living at Qumran near the Dead Sea anticipated two messiahs. The community was to govern itself by a strict rule, doing so until the coming of "the Messiahs of Aaron and Israel."[1] In other words, they awaited the emergence of both a priestly messiah and a royal one.

While retaining messianic hope, other groups refashioned it circumstantially. Those zealous for a military revolution against the Romans thrust possible kingly messiahs forward. We know about them from the Jewish historian Josephus, who wrote shortly after the time of Jesus. They include men such as Judas the Galilean, Simon (a servant of Herod), Anthroges, Menahem, and Simon bar Giora.[2] They were not Davidic, so they did not quite fit the bill in terms of what God had promised. But since they were powerful leaders ready to hand, certain revolutionaries were willing to press their messianic claims.

But God had made specific promises that bounded the fluidity, so for most Jews the primary messianic hope remained royal and Davidic. This is why the Gospels in the New Testament announce that Jesus is born into the line of David. It fulfills prophecy. But upon his birth, Jesus did not fulfill the messianic hope immediately.

Jesus announced the good news as an *unfolding process*: God's heavenly rule was beginning to impinge on the earth in an unexpected way. It was like a seed that would grow in an unexpected fashion (Matt. 13:1–43; Mark 4:1–34). As we shall see, Jesus's rescuing kingship includes the cross, resurrection, and much more.

But here's the point I want to drive home: God's ultimate salvation comes not simply through Jesus, but through Jesus in his specific capacity as the one enthroned at God's right hand. From that position he is governing God's new creation work. Jesus's saving benefits are available only because he is first and foremost the King.

The King Proclaims Himself

While John the Baptist was still preaching, Jesus of Nazareth began his public ministry by "proclaiming the gospel of God" (Mark 1:14, AT). Don't miss it! Jesus himself was a herald of the gospel *before* his death.

Any valid explanation of the gospel's content and purposes must be able to explain how and why Jesus announced the gospel *prior to* his death for sins. That is, although Jesus's gospel ultimately included the cross and forgiveness in anticipation of those events, it can't have referred exclusively to those events. Jesus was summoning hearers to repentance and a faith commitment as a present-tense response to the gospel some three years before his death.

Jesus's gospel proclamation was not primarily about trusting in his death to obtain personal forgiveness of sin. What gospel did Jesus proclaim? "The time has been fulfilled and the kingdom of God has drawn near" (Mark 1:15, AT). *The basic framework for the gospel is "the kingdom of God."* However the cross and resurrection fit into the gospel—and they are indeed integral to it—we must contextualize them within an announcement of good news as that pertains to God's broader kingdom purposes.

More precisely the content of Jesus's gospel pertains to *the fulfilment of time* and *the nearness of the kingdom of God.* How can we unpack Jesus's exact meaning? Allowing Scripture to interpret Scripture, we can look for clues elsewhere. An ideal passage to help us understand Jesus's words will include (1) gospel language, (2) Jesus speaking about the fulfillment of time, (3) Jesus explaining the nearness of the kingdom of God, and (4) Jesus interpreting his own ministry with respect to John the Baptist's.

Consider Luke 7:17–28. Jesus's ministry was attracting attention and opposition. Meanwhile John the Baptist had been thrown in prison for telling Herod that it was unlawful to divorce his wife in order to run off with his half-brother Philip's wife. Herod's wife swap was so notorious that it is described not only in the Bible (Luke 3:19–20); it is also recounted in much greater detail by Josephus.[3]

While John was in prison for confronting Herod, John sent two of his disciples to ask Jesus: "Are you *the coming one,* or should we expect someone else?" (Luke 7:20, AT). This question about *the coming one* is an oblique way of asking whether Jesus is in fact the royal messiah (see Luke 19:38). John had already identified Jesus as the coming messiah (Luke 3:15–17), but given the discouraging circumstances, John had begun to harbor doubts.

Luke describes the cleverly pointed way in which Jesus sought to assuage John's fears:

> At that very time Jesus cured many who had diseases, sicknesses and evil spirits, and gave sight to many who were blind. So he

replied to the messengers, "Go back and report to John what you have seen and heard: The blind receive sight, the lame walk, those who have leprosy are cleansed, the deaf hear, the dead are raised, and *the gospel* is proclaimed to the poor. Blessed is anyone who does not stumble on account of me." (Luke 7:21–24, NIV, slightly modified)

Jesus's active ministry provides the foundation for his reply to John. Jesus indicates that the substance of his ministry proves that he is indeed the long-awaited "coming one," the royal king. Jesus declares that his own activities are a gospel proclamation (see also Luke 4:16–21).

In short, Jesus announces that he is the coming king. Nevertheless, his reply to John is oblique. Jesus wants John to know he is indeed the emerging king—and that the signs of his reign are blossoming all around for those who have eyes to see—but he prefers to say this indirectly at that moment given the tense political dynamic between John and "King" Herod. (Herod was really only a tetrarch but craved the title "king.") If Jesus were to say, "I am the coming messiah" in this context, it would be an affront to Herod's royal pretensions (see Matt. 11:8–15; Luke 16:16–18). It might result in Jesus's premature execution.

In a fascinating archaeological discovery we find proof that some were expecting God to accomplish in the messiah's day *exactly* what Jesus told John that he was doing. The Dead Sea Scrolls, written just prior to the time of Jesus by a group living about 20 miles from Jerusalem, express these hopes:

> For the heavens and the earth shall listen to his Messiah . . . the fruit of good deeds shall not be delayed for anyone and the Lord shall do glorious things which have not been done, just as He said. For He shall heal the critically wounded, He shall revive the dead, He shall send good news [*gospel*] to the afflicted, He shall satisfy the poor, He shall guide the uprooted, He shall make the hungry rich.[4]

Notice the uncanny similarities between this community's hope for a long-awaited messiah and Jesus's description of his own ministry: healings, raisings of the dead, gospel proclaimed to the afflicted, the poor and hungry satiated. A transition is envisioned from the present era to a new epoch in which the goodness of God's reign is immediate and transparent through the messiah's rule. The Dead Sea Scrolls help confirm what we already see in the Bible: Jesus's gospel was a self-proclamation that he was the coming messiah, the king.

In short, what it meant for Jesus to preach the gospel was for him to announce that he—not Herod or any of his ilk—was God's anointed king and that he would bring about the gospel announced in Isaiah of God's reign—that is, God's sovereign heaven-meets-earth rule. Jesus was the chosen messiah and he would attain full enthronement despite haughty "kings" like Herod who pretend to rule on God's behalf.

The Rescuing King

As the anointed King-in-waiting, Jesus was already undertaking royal action in behalf of the poor, broken, and imprisoned in anticipation of his attainment of the scepter officially. One day he would occupy the throne fully, ruling completely on God's behalf—reversing wrongs. In other words, he announced and showed that God's new empire was arriving through his own royal presence.

Now we begin to discover why Jesus's kingship is truly the good news humanity needs. As part of our common humanity, we all are afflicted by a damaging tendency to ignore God's wise kingship and to rule ourselves. Here is the basic human condition in a nutshell: I want *what I want* and I will pursue it regardless of what God says about what is good for me and for others.

Given we are trapped within a damaging self-rule, God's rescue doesn't merely involve forgiveness for our past mistakes. As N. T. Wright points out, "Good news creates a new situation and calls for new decisions."[5] It means deliverance into a fundamentally different situation. Salvation includes a new situation, the restoration of God's proper rule over humans.

Jesus was saving by creating an avenue through which God's heaven-based rule could be experienced by humans in its fullness once again. The restoration of God's reign over humanity is not something extra beyond salvation from our sins. *Jesus's kingship—in all it entails—is how humans are being saved from their sins.*

Jesus's gospel message was an announcement of his kingship. It was central to his mission. In fact, when launching his public ministry, Jesus identifies it as the fundamental *why*—the most basic reason that the Father sent him. After healing the sick and exorcising evil spirits in Capernaum, the people tried to prevent him from ever leaving. But Jesus, after praying in a solitary place, told them, "I must proclaim *the gospel of the kingdom of God* to the other towns also, *because that is why I was sent*" (Luke 4:43).

Why the gospel? Jesus's own answer to that question is that he was sent to proclaim the good news about his *kingship*.

The Emerging King

Jesus and the apostles preached the same gospel but from different horizons in history. In the Gospels, Jesus's gospel message is that *the kingdom of God has drawn near*, because Jesus is announcing that he is in the process of fully becoming the Messiah. As we shall see, in Acts and the rest of the New Testament, the gospel is that *Jesus is the Messiah (or the Christ)* because once he ascended to the right hand of the Father, the process of Jesus becoming the Messiah was then complete. Jesus had then become the Christ in the fullest sense.

We can describe the whole process by which Jesus became the Messiah this way: As the eternal Son he was chosen by God before the foundation of the world as the future king (Eph. 1:4–5). He takes on human flesh for this purpose. But in terms of history, the becoming-the-messiah process formally began when Jesus was anointed ("christened") at his baptism, making him "the Christ." At this time he was the messiah-in-waiting because he did not yet rule officially from a throne. As the king-in-waiting he already exercised royal authority—as evidenced by his mighty deeds—albeit in a preliminary fashion. Yet he had not been installed in his official office as the Messiah. It was necessary that he experience death and resurrection first, winning the victory over sin and death on our behalf. Then he ascended to God's right hand where he was granted an *eternal throne* in fulfillment of God's promises.[6]

When Jesus sat down at the right hand of the Father, he began to wield all God's authority as the fully divine and fully human king. Then he was the Messiah completely and officially.

Cross and Resurrection Instead?

What about the cross and resurrection? Perhaps you are on board with the need to emphasize Jesus's kingship as a key gospel claim. But you are not convinced yet that it is the *primary* purpose of the gospel. Jesus as King, you may be thinking, is all very well. But surely the cross has a greater claim to primacy as pure gospel. The resurrection too.

Are you sure? Can you prove from the Bible that the cross and resurrection are more foundational to the gospel than Jesus's kingship? I challenge you. Go ahead. Assemble evidence that the cross and resurrection are more essential to the gospel than kingship.

I'll wait here. . . .

Done?

Let's see what you came up with.

Perhaps you weighed Paul's strong words: "For Christ did not send me to baptize, but to preach the gospel—not with wisdom and eloquence, lest the cross of Christ be emptied of its power. For the message of the cross is foolishness to those who are perishing, but to us who are being saved it is the power of God" (1 Cor. 1:17–18,

NIV). This is a poignant reminder that the cross is inescapably part of the gospel. It is indeed. Amen.

But did you notice? Or did you fall into the habit of treating *Christ* as a name rather than a royal title? Paul says that *the Christ* sent him to preach the gospel in the first place. Second, the gospel does indeed involve the cross—but Paul does not describe it simply as the cross nor as the cross of Jesus. Rather it is the *cross of the Christ*. In other words, in this passage Paul presupposes that Jesus has become the Christ to such a degree that it is the enthroned King who sends his servants to preach the gospel in the first place, and once they are sent, the message of *the cross* is further described as *of the Christ*. Paul's words about the gospel and the cross here are both informed and qualified by Jesus's kingship.

In other words, it is true that we should always and everywhere "preach Christ crucified" (1 Cor. 1:22), but we dare not forget that *the Christ*, the King—not the cross—is given primacy as the one preached. Meanwhile the *crucified* qualifies what type of king is in view. Kingship is the scaffolding within which the work of the cross is contextualized as gospel in the New Testament.

Perhaps you pondered 1 Corinthians 15 as you thought about passages that prioritize death and resurrection, since it contains the most explicit description of the gospel in the Bible. It says that the gospel Paul received and transmitted is "that *the Christ* died for our sins in accordance with the Scriptures, that he was buried, that he has been raised on the third day in accordance with the Scriptures, and that he appeared to Cephas, and then to the Twelve" (1 Cor. 15:3–5, AT). There it is again: "*the Christ.*"

Here Paul indicates that Jesus's attainment of kingship is the gospel's essential framework before even speaking about what happened at the cross or about the resurrection. Paul doesn't say Jesus of Nazareth died for our sins. He says *the Christ* died. He doesn't say Jesus was raised. He says *the Messiah* was raised. In Paul's clearest presentation of the gospel, he points us to Jesus's attained messianic office—his kingship—as the proper framework for understanding the cross and resurrection.

That Jesus has become the Christ is essential to the gospel. But our instinct to prioritize Jesus's death and resurrection as especially critical to the gospel is also sound. Paul identifies four events in his description of the gospel in 1 Corinthians 15:3–5—death, burial, resurrection, and appearances to witnesses. Elsewhere Paul identifies other events as part of the gospel too. But Paul's arrangement shows that he believed death and resurrection to have great theological heft.

Only the Christ's death and resurrection are "according to the Scriptures"—that is, anticipated in the Old Testament. Moreover, the Christ's death for sins is proven by burial and resurrection by appearances, not vice versa. The cross and resurrection are indeed essential to the gospel. But we can't miss *kingship*. That Jesus has become the Christ is presupposed as the gospel framework within which the work of the cross and the resurrection have meaning.

A supplemental passage makes it explicit that death and resurrection were not the endgame but ultimately were purposed toward something even more climactic: Jesus's attainment of ruling authority. Paul declares, "For this very reason, the Christ died and returned to life *so that he might be the Lord of both the dead and the living*" (Rom. 14:9–12, AT). Here the purpose of the cross and resurrection is Jesus's attainment of sovereignty over the dead and the living.

This passage is especially helpful, because it puts death for sins and resurrection from the dead within Scripture's wider story: *Jesus's death and resurrection were not ends in and of themselves but led to Jesus's sovereign rule.* Once Jesus attained sovereign rule through the cross and resurrection, then the benefits of the cross and resurrection could be bestowed on the basis of his royal and high priestly authority.

Why Kingship Must Come First

We are not given something else prior, like forgiveness or regeneration, in the gospel, so that subsequently we can submit to Jesus's kingship. The King himself is first. Several years ago, in a series of posts hosted by *9Marks* and *Christianity Today*, respectively, a pastor carried out a back-and-forth discussion with Scot McKnight and me about the gospel. This pastor (or his editor) gave one of his articles the brazen title "'Jesus is King' Is Not Good News."

To be candid, Scot and I found the title shocking. Many others did too. Given the Bible repeatedly summarizes the good news by asserting that Jesus is the Christ—which means the King—there was considerable social-media backlash. Quickly the pastor (or his editor) changed the title. This was prudent, for it would be hard to formulate a title that more blatantly disregards Scripture's preferred way of speaking about the gospel. Jesus's attainment of the kingship is the very essence of the good news in the Bible. First we receive the grace of the Christ as the fundamental gospel reality (see Acts 5:42; 9:22; 17:2–3; cf. Gal. 1:6; Acts 20:24). It is only *after* his kingship has been graciously established that we can respond to the gospel's fullness, so that we share in the saving benefits that the King bestows.[7]

Other passages help us make sense of why kingship is the most basic purpose of the gospel—even while the cross, resurrection, and other events are equally essential to its fullness. When we attend to Scripture with care, we discover that the cross and resurrection were purposed toward an even more ultimate aim: giving us a king, *so that the cross-and-resurrection benefits that attend his kingship* can be experienced. As Peter puts it, "God exalted him [Jesus] to his own right hand as Prince and Savior that he might bring Israel to repentance and forgive their sins" (Acts 5:31, AT). Notice the pattern: first rule at the right hand, then repentance and forgiveness.

In other words, we can't pretend as if the cross and resurrection work in isolation. Their power depends on Jesus's attainment of full sovereignty. There is no forgiveness for ultimate salvation apart from the establishment and reality of Jesus's kingship first. It was necessary that Jesus *be exalted to God's right hand*, his position as the head of new creation—King of kings and High Priest—for the forgiveness of final salvation to issue forth.

This is also why when elsewhere Peter preaches about Jesus's death and resurrection, his sermon reaches a climax not there, but with what happened next—Jesus's attainment of the ultimate position of royal authority: "God has made this Jesus, whom you crucified, both Lord and Messiah" (Acts 2:36). Once again, it is not on the basis of the cross and resurrection alone that forgiveness is offered. Rather, first Jesus had to receive the throne at God's right hand. Once he has sovereign power as the crucified-and-raised King, he then has the authority to offer clemency. So Peter declares, "Repent and be baptized for the forgiveness of your sins" (Acts 2:38).

Responding to Jesus's Kingship

We are saved when we respond to the gospel of Jesus the King. To understand what that entails, we must appreciate grace and faith. The term "grace" (*charis*) is frequently presented in ways that sound biblical but are inadequate. The best studies of *charis* in the New Testament and its world show that the concept of grace is multifaceted, since within a patron–client system gifts vary in size, purpose, timing, the degree to which they are merited, intended effects, and final benefits.[8]

Yet when speaking of final salvation, we can summarize by saying the gospel itself is God's premier grace (Acts 20:24; Gal. 1:6). God gave saving grace, the good news of the gift of the Messiah, to humanity as a whole some two thousand years ago even though humans had done nothing to deserve it (Eph. 2:1–10). Meanwhile saving grace does not leave us helpless. It changes us, so we become increasingly like our King (Rom. 5:17; 2 Cor. 12:9). Saving grace is effective for bringing about final transformation as the Spirit supplies the gospel's benefits to those who express "faith" so that they are "in" King Jesus (Eph. 1:3–14). Through these God-initiated processes, the gift of the gospel is still God's saving grace today.

Since the gospel emphasizes God's gracious gift of Jesus as King, each person must respond with a commitment of "faith" or "allegiance" (*pistis*) to Jesus as King or Lord in order for the gospel to become effective for personal salvation (Rom. 10:9–10; 2 Thess. 1:4–8). In the New Testament although *pistis* has a mental and volitional dimension, it is primarily an outward-facing relational term.[9] As Nijay Gupta puts it, "Obeying faith is relationally active: faithfulness is understood in this discussion as an active form of loyalty and obedience."[10] That is, "faith" is something you demonstrate toward another through your bodily actions that express trust, faithfulness, obedience, loyalty, and allegiance. As James so memorably states in his letter, "As the body without the spirit is dead, so faith without deeds is dead" (2:26). Saving faith includes deeds of allegiance as part of its embodied expression.

A person is saved not simply by trusting in Jesus as Savior but by pledging "faith" (allegiance) to the Christ-King. Normally the way to confess faith to Jesus as King is through repentance from previous sinful loyalties and through baptism.

Baptism into Jesus as *the Christ* recognizes that the Father sent the Son to take on human flesh and that he died for sins, was raised, was enthroned at the right hand as the eternal King, sent the Holy Spirit, and will return to rule. In this way baptism into the name of Jesus as the Christ summarizes and safeguards the King Jesus gospel in much the same way as baptism into the name of the Father, Son, and the Holy Spirit. It is no surprise that the New Testament emphasizes both (for example, Acts 2:38; 8:16; Matt. 28:19).

The gospel reveals the two greatest Christian mysteries: the incarnate King and the Trinity. Our baptism is an allegiant response to King Jesus, the Son who stands at the heart of these mysteries both as the revealer and the one revealed. Personal salvation only comes by a commitment, however imperfect, to give allegiance to King Jesus.

Let's not repeat past church mistakes by pretending the gospel is about something else first—like accepting Jesus as Savior for forgiveness—and then responding to his lordship or kingship secondarily. If a person hasn't pledged faith to Jesus as King or Lord, then they have not yet responded to the gospel in its fullness so as to receive forgiveness and liberation. Never forget: *the gospel is king first.*

Why the Gospel?

Because we need a king.

After leaving Canada, back in my hometown in California, my wife and I settled into routines. Forestry work was honest, but in my immaturity I was embarrassed to return to my high school job. I felt called to teach Scripture. I somehow managed to finish my master's degree at Regent College over distance (this was in the early 2000s, before online education was a viable option). Yet the prospect of a professional teaching career was tenuous.

A friend who was a top-notch video game programmer gave me the chance to learn the craft from him. I had intermediate programming skills, but it would take months, perhaps a year, to get up to sufficient speed. Here's the thing: although there is nothing inherently wrong with video games, at least many of them, I knew this didn't align with the unshakeable dreams God had laid on my heart. Plus, I'm not even good at video games. But I took my friend up on his offer.

I failed to trust, ignored God's call, and took charge of my future career. The King had given me a specific vocation and tasks. But I was afraid to have no "real" career prospects. So I hedged my bets. It was my attempt to mitigate social embarrassment and enter a respectable career in case my true calling didn't pan out.

It failed miserably. I spent half a year learning, but it never went anywhere. I tried to force open another window by crawling back to my electrical-engineering career, even though I hated the work and the hour-long commute. It drained every ounce of joy from my body. Had I trusted, the forestry job would have supplied our needs and allowed ample free time. The year and a half I spent bouncing between programming and engineering rather than working in forestry could have been used to teach Scripture locally and train for future ministry. Huge waste.

In exercising my own sovereignty, it was not that I had ceased to be a committed Christian. Nor had I failed to trust Jesus's saving power. I simply had not yet learned the main purpose of the gospel in theory let alone in practice. Something redemptive did emerge through it in the end. I learned a key gospel truth, albeit in an upside-down fashion: *I am a horrible king of my own life.*

It was the start I needed. Eventually it would propel me toward healing—a process still unfolding. I have much more to say about the purpose of the gospel. But I found out the hard way that we must begin with the one essential: the good news is that God has provided a king.

The gospel is king first. We think the main reason God has given us the gospel is to help us because we are trapped in sin. Or that the gospel is given because we need forgiveness. We are trapped in sin, and we do need forgiveness, but these secondary purposes can only flow from the primary one. As far as Scripture is concerned, the essence of the gospel is the gift of a king. We dare not ever forget it, because when we begin to experience Jesus's kingship, it is better news than we could have ever imagined.

QUESTIONS FOR DISCUSSION OR REFLECTION

1. Describe a time when you let yourself reign without paying attention to God's sovereignty over your life.
2. With regard to what you receive *first* through the gospel, what has been emphasized in your past experiences with church traditions or evangelism?
3. Why is it imperative to recognize that Scripture emphasizes that the gospel is *king* first?
4. How does the meaning of the song "In Christ alone, my hope

is found" change if "Christ" is allowed to mean more than simply "Jesus"?

5. The book suggests four ways to help remind ourselves and others that Jesus Christ is not a name. Which do you find most helpful? Can you think of other ways?

6. Why is it vital to know that the Christ is announced in the Old Testament? Should this affect how we present the gospel today?

7. Can you describe the process by which Jesus fully became the Christ?

8. Why is it important to recognize that Jesus's becoming the Christ was not instantaneous but was instead a historical process? How does this change what it means for you to respond to Jesus?

9. What gospel did Jesus proclaim? How does this compare with your previous understandings of the gospel's content?

10. How should we respond to the claim that the cross and resurrection are more important to the gospel than Jesus's kingship? Why?

11. How do grace and faith interface with the gospel of Jesus's kingship?

12. What is a saving response to the gospel? How does the gospel relate to baptism?

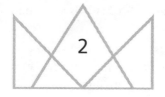

Famous Somewhere

"When everybody loves me, then I'll never be lonely." Adam Duritz and Marty Jones were drunk in a bar. They noticed a well-known drummer on the other side of the room. He had managed to captivate three gorgeous women in a conversation by his charms. Or more likely, so they thought, by his fame.

Duritz and Jones were unknown musicians. One day they would be famous too, they dreamed. Then everything would be easy: self-confidence, music, girls, money. Duritz went home from the bar and wrote a song that includes the lyric above and other declarations that express a yearning for fame: "When I look at the television, I want to see me staring right back at me." The song expresses a deeply held conviction that stardom will lead to happiness.

Ironically, this song, "Mr. Jones," would be the smash radio single that would skyrocket Duritz's band, Counting Crows, to the front of the indie music scene in the 1990s.[1] He got what he wanted. Or did he?

The sparkle of fame. It's alluring. Even if we don't want to be Lady Gaga, Leonardo DiCaprio, or Steph Curry—celebrity might prove to be a hassle—we yearn to be significant, to be recognized, to be known. For most of us, if we're honest, when we post on Twitter, Facebook, and Instagram, beyond all else we are guided by the mantra: *See me!* It seems to be programmed into our DNA. We desperately want to matter.

Good news! It is a God-given desire. Moreover, God has done something to make it happen. Did you know a primary and repeated purpose of the gospel in Scripture is to make you famous?

Wait a second, you say, is this one of those health-and-wealth gospel books? Nope. You'll find ample take-up-your-cross-and-follow in this book. But seriously, a key purpose of the gospel in the Bible is to make you famous. Me too.

More on that in a moment.

First, we need to secure the foundations by closing off false trails. The most basic purpose of the gospel is to give us a king. But you'll often hear other versions of the gospel that advance faulty purposes. In what follows, I present six malformed gospels that remain popular today.

Six Malformed Gospels and Purposes

The church can take steps toward a better future by safeguarding itself against past and present mistakes. Here are six versions of the gospel and their accompanying purposes that have been popular among Christians for generations. Each is still prevalent today even among mature Christians and in otherwise good churches.

I call these six "malformed gospels" because each has elements of truth—some more, some less. But if Scripture is the standard, they all fail to identify the true content and purpose of the gospel accurately. They are misshapen. Let's consider what is wrong with each of them.

The Believe-for-Heaven Malformed Gospel

The believe-for-heaven misshapen gospel describes the bad news this way: God only wants you to believe in Jesus as your personal Savior, but people can't seem to accept this simple truth, so they are always adding other requirements.

Advocates for this distorted view of the gospel tend to think as follows: You can only be saved by believing personally that Jesus died for your sins. Jesus is Lord, but that is not relevant for your salvation. If you think you need to commit to obeying Jesus in any fashion to be saved, you've interjected your own doing into the process. You've compromised God's grace by conditioning it. The gospel is that God wants to save you purely through believing the all-important singular fact about the universe: Jesus died for your sins.

This malformed gospel's purpose is to get you to believe so you can go to heaven.

The Freedom-from-Rules Malformed Gospel

The freedom-from-rules misshapen gospel contends that the bad news is this: people keep imposing their values and rules on me and others. These people say that a truly good person—a true Christian—wouldn't drink, cuss, wear "that" shirt, get body piercings, or watch certain movies. The coercive pressure of their false values is horrible for me and for Christianity.

Those who embrace this distorted gospel describe it as follows: the good news is that Jesus shows us that legalistic rule-makers are misguided. Jesus hung out with sinners and had harsh words for those who judged. So no true Christian could ever tell someone else how to behave. Not only are those who impose rules wrong, they also are hypocrites. Those telling others not to watch certain movies are secretly doing worse things in the dark. Jesus came to set each person free from rules, rule-makers, and legalistic religious nonsense. Jesus frees each individual to live in light of his or her own conscience before God.

This distorted gospel's purpose is to create a tolerant society by ending the tyranny of rules and judgmentalism, so we all can enjoy uninhibited personal freedom.

The Stop-Striving-and-Rest Malformed Gospel

The bad news within the stop-striving-and-rest misshapen gospel is that you are constantly trying to earn God's favor by *doing*. Yet you still feel inadequate.

Adherents of this deformed gospel suggest that the good news is that God wants to set you free from performance. All you need to do is trust that there is absolutely nothing you could ever do to earn God's favor, but that Jesus has earned it for you. Jesus performs perfectly on your behalf. Once you trust in the grace found in Jesus—really trust—you are set free from your perceived need to earn God's approval—or anyone else's. You can finally rest secure in the knowledge that you are loved by God for who you are in him, not for your performance. In your newfound freedom, you'll be more in love with Jesus than ever, so now you'll want to do good deeds not to earn favor but as an expression of your gratitude.

This malformed gospel's purpose is to get you to realize that if you truly trust in Jesus, you are accepted for his sake rather than for your achievements, so you can finally relax.

The Improve-Society Malformed Gospel

Within this distorted gospel, the bad news is the world is filled with meanness, evil, and violence. I can't fix the world's problems—they are too big.

The good news is my friends and I are mostly on the right track. At least we have the right ideals, agenda, and social activism. We are trying to fix these problems and help others. Usually. True, sometimes we compromise our own values and make wrong choices. But it can hardly be helped; the whole system is corrupt.

Devotees of this improve-society distorted gospel look to Jesus for social renewal: Jesus casts a vision for the perfect society—one that will help the poor, end violence, and respect diversity.

This deformed gospel's purpose is to get everyone to embrace Jesus's nonjudgmental, love-the-sinner, accept-the-outsider, turn-the-other-cheek ideals so together we can create a more just, diverse, and tolerant society.

The Reunion-with-God Malformed Gospel

The reunion-with-God misshapen gospel focuses on seeking to recover intimacy with God. Humans were originally in God's presence. But Adam and Eve sinned, so the bad news is we are eternally separated from a righteous God because of our sins.

The reunion-with-God malformed gospel stresses the need to be reestablished in a right relationship with God so that we can enter his presence once again: the good news is that Jesus has carried your sins for you, so if you put your faith in him and him alone, your sins can be forgiven. Pray a sinner's prayer and make a decision to trust Jesus to be your personal Savior. Now you are right with God not because you are righteous, but because Jesus's righteousness has been credited to your account. Now you are free to grow in holiness. But most important, you'll get to be with God forever.

This deformed gospel's purpose is to get you to trust in Jesus's righteousness rather than your own so you can enjoy God's presence forever.

The Participate-in-the-Sacraments Malformed Gospel

According to the deformed participate-in-the-sacraments version of the gospel, the bad news is sin prevents people from joining the church and following its heavenward procedures.

For those who advance this distorted version of it, the gospel is that God has provided a sure pathway to final salvation if you participate in the saving practices Jesus gave his church. A hyper-sacramentalist might express the gospel as follows: You can do nothing to earn the grace of the sacraments, but God gives them to you freely as a gift. They are effective automatically when they are carried out by the church personnel God has approved to perform them. You must be baptized by a person who uses the right words and actions. Subsequently you must be confirmed, partake in communion, and participate in required church fasts, feasts, and other activities. When you fall short you must confess your sins to a priest in hope that your sins can be absolved, reconciling you to God. The good news is that if you follow these sacramental procedures, God promises that you will get to go to heaven.

This distorted gospel's purpose is to get you to participate in the saving sacraments under the authority of approved personnel, for through these God promises to guide you to heaven.

What Is Wrong with These Malformed Gospels?

Each of the six malformed gospels presented above touches on the truth. Some more, some less. But there are also problems. A fun and interesting task would be to identify what is uniquely good and ill in each of the six skewed gospels presented above.[2] Even more deformed varieties could have been listed too—such as the *health-and-wealth gospel* or the *Jesus-affirms-but-never-corrects-me gospel*. But beyond specific missteps, did you notice problems common to all six?

The Missing King

None of these six popular but malformed versions of the gospel feature what Scripture presents as its very essence—*Jesus is the Christ*. Elements of these misshapen gospels may be compatible with the true gospel of Jesus's kingship if massaged and repackaged. But none make Jesus's *royal* authority as the Christ, and its acknowledgment, required as the first stage of salvation. None make acceptance of his kingship a priority.

The seriousness of this error cannot be overstated. As biblical scholar Scot McKnight reminds us, the true gospel is "the *King Jesus Gospel*."[3] To miss Jesus as *King* is to miss the gospel entirely.

The Missing Storyline

The absence of *King* Jesus is the first and the most dangerous error in the six malformed gospels discussed above. Yet there are other significant problems.

Second, the full gospel has a storied shape. But the six malformed gospels presented above fail to track that story accurately or otherwise have gaping holes, so that crucial elements of the gospel are missing. None of the six holistically draws on *all* the essential facets of the biblical gospel's content—incarnation, death for sins, resurrection, enthronement as everlasting King, Spirit-sending, and royal return—when identifying the gospel's content or purpose. The biblical gospel has a specific narrative shape, a storyline.

We'll have more opportunity to explore why it is necessary to uphold the full storyline of the gospel—including quite specific elements of that story—if we are to understand its most precise purposes as this book unfolds. At this juncture it is sufficient to see that these six versions of the gospel are deformed because the good news in Scripture is not simply *Jesus* first. The gospel is *King Jesus* first—and it has a specific Trinitarian storyline that includes essential elements.

Missing Allegiance

Not only is kingship absent and the storied content of these six gospels misshapen, but you also may have noticed a third problem in them. They all emphasize that the gospel demands a response to Jesus, but none require *allegiance* to the King as the gospel's main response and purpose. They all suggest the gospel is purposed toward something—release from hell, attainment of heaven, righteousness, forgiveness, freedom from striving, improvement of society, reunion with God, or an approved salvation procedure. But none stress that the gospel's basic purpose is loyalty to King Jesus.

Allegiance matters. We are called to respond with loyal obedience to the good news that God has installed Jesus as King of the universe. The clearest statements about the purpose of the gospel in Scripture can be found in Romans, phrased the exact same way both times. The gospel of Jesus the Christ is "for the obedience of faith in all the nations" (Rom. 1:5; 16:26). Since the context involves responding to Jesus as *Christ* and *Lord* (Rom. 1:4–8), the phrase "for the obedience of faith" (*eis hypakoēn pisteōs*) is best further translated *allegiant obedience* or *loyal obedience*. The required response to the gospel in the Bible coincides with its purpose: allegiance to King Jesus.

Why the gospel? *The gospel's clearest purpose in Scripture is bodily allegiance to King Jesus in every nation.*

Missing Fame

There is a fourth element that is missing in these six malformed gospels. We have not yet discussed it, but it is a major purpose of the gospel in Scripture. None highlight the restoration of *fame*.

What has fame to do with the gospel? Everything! If this isn't better known, it is because of language issues. The problem isn't just that we speak English while the Old Testament is written in Hebrew and Aramaic. Or that the New Testament is in Greek. We speak a different language altogether.

The obscure language we speak in church is called *Christianese*. Words that originally had nothing to do with the church—for example, *baptize*—over time came to have distinctly religious overtones.

In the New Testament era, you baptize a garment to dye it. You baptize metal in water to temper it. A ship that is sinking is being baptized. It was not a religious word. It meant to dip or immerse. But over time, through Christianity's impact, a religious meaning came to predominate. Today it would seem irreverent to speak of baptizing your donut in your coffee before eating it. Not so when Jesus and the apostles lived.

Becoming Famous

To grasp all that God is trying to tell us in Scripture, we need to undo the Christianese.

Consider *glory*. When we're speaking Christianese to one another, then *glory* evokes certain images: heaven, overwhelming light, a chorus of angels, brightness, radiance, splendor, beauty, final victory, white wings, and golden crowns. The Greek word *doxa*, which is usually translated *glory* in our Bibles, has some of these associations in the New Testament. But if you were to crack open the leading Greek dictionary that covers the New Testament and its world, you would discover that *doxa* pertains to *greatness, fame, recognition, renown, honor,* and *prestige.*[4]

In the New Testament, glory means not so much heavenly brightness but *fame.* The same is true for glory in the Old Testament, in which the word *kabod* intimates weightiness. We sense a weight of presence—heft, power, greatness, clout—when we are near a well-known person, so *kabod* ordinarily means fame in the Old Testament too. Although we can be misled by our Christianese to think glory is purely about heavenly splendor, glory in the Bible is bound up with reputation, regard, honor—and yes, fame.

Why the gospel? A consistent reason Scripture gives is *glory* or *fame.* Through the gospel God wants to make you famous—to enhance your ultimate reputation.

But before trying to land a Kardashianesque reality TV show, tread carefully. Adam Duritz longed to be a megastar. But after his meteoric rise, he discovered fame's dark side. Let's not start promoting brand *me* to the world quite yet. Instead let's learn more about God-style fame. It probably won't surprise you to learn that the fame that God intends for you through the gospel is different from and far better than the world's shabby imitation.

Gospel Fame

A concise description of the gospel is given by Paul in his second letter to Timothy. "Remember Jesus the Christ, having been raised from amid those who are dead, of the seed of David—according to my gospel" (2 Tim. 2:8, AT). We'll have more to say about how the New Testament summarizes the gospel in a subsequent chapter. Here we are interested in what we can learn about the gospel's purpose. What Paul says next is instructive. But first, some context.

The gospel was priceless to Paul. We know this because when Paul wrote this letter, he was in prison for preaching it. Actually, it was worse. Paul knew the time of his departure had come—that he was about to be executed (4:6). He had finished the race (4:7). Indeed, we learn from sources outside the Bible that Paul was executed by the emperor Nero not long after penning this letter.[5]

Since death's shadow was stretching over Paul even as he wrote, his words to Timothy about the gospel are poignant: "This is my gospel," Paul declares, "for which I am suffering even to the point of being chained like a criminal" (2:8–9, NIV). Yet despite his suffering, Paul affirmed "God's word is not chained" (2:9, NIV). That is, he knew that God's gospel cannot be imprisoned. Paul had learned that hardships, like imprisonment, actually serve to "advance the gospel" (Phil. 1:12, AT). Official attempts to stifle God's good news only make it bound forth more readily.

After outlining the content of the gospel for Timothy, Paul explains why he is willing to go to prison for its sake. In so doing, he speaks about the gospel's purpose: "Therefore I endure everything for the sake of the elect, that they too may obtain the salvation that is in the Christ, Jesus, *with eternal glory*" (2 Tim. 2:10, AT).

Did you catch that? "With *eternal glory*." Press past the Christianese. A key purpose of the gospel is salvation in the King, Jesus, but along with that comes reputation, honor, fame. One of the reasons God gave the gospel was so that our reputation will be enhanced in an everlasting fashion.

In some Christian circles we are browbeaten to think our thirst to be highly regarded by others—for significance, reputation, fame—is perverse. We think fame is something that we need to die to as Christians. But that is a half-truth. For what Scripture says about the gospel's purpose proves that God will satisfy our hunger for a great reputation. We will attain everlasting honor. How? And what exactly might that look like?

The very next verses hint at an answer. But at this stage, we aren't ready for the main course, so consider Paul's words to be an appetizer: "Here is a trustworthy saying: If we died with him, we will also live with him; if we endure, we will also reign with him" (2 Tim. 2:11–12, AT). God intends everlasting honor for us through the gospel. But whatever that might mean, it cannot be separated from an intimate identification with King Jesus.

Whatever fame we will enjoy will come through a participation in the Christ's death, so that we might find life. It will require that

God intends everlasting honor for us through the gospel.

we persevere with the King, so that we can participate in his royal rule over a renewed creation. More on that toward the end of this book. Right now, let's probe further into how Scripture speaks about the relationship between gospel and glory.

This next example is interesting, because at first it is not clear that Paul is speaking about the purpose of the gospel at all. But then we discover it is his main point.

In a letter written to the suffering church in Thessalonica, Paul expresses gratitude for how God has been at work in their midst: "But we ought always to thank God for you, brothers and sisters loved by the Lord, because God chose you as firstfruits to be saved through the sanctifying work of the Spirit and through belief in the truth" (2 Thess. 2:14, AT). In other words, Paul expresses confidence that those who are following the Lord Jesus in Thessalonica have been chosen by God as the firstfruits—the first installment. This means they are among the first to be ingathered as part of his saving harvest, and that a greater ingathering will follow. As the first to be gathered, Paul reminds the Thessalonians that despite their hardships, they have been set apart by God as his holy people by the Holy Spirit and by their adherence to God's truth.

Then, Paul reveals how God's saving actions—choosing and sanctifying the community—relate to the purpose of the gospel: "He called you to this *through our gospel,* that you might *share in the glory* of our Lord Jesus Christ" (2 Thess. 2:13, NIV). Again, the purpose of the gospel is that we might join in the glory. The choosing and sanctifying as part of the salvation process are not ends in themselves, but are purposed toward a greater end through the gospel: *sharing in the glory of the Lord Jesus, the Christ.* A fundamental purpose of the gospel is our glory—that is, our fame, honor, and good reputation.

Yet it is *glory together.* If we are narcissistic enough to think that the fame and honor that God intends for us are about brand *me,* this passage should disabuse us of any such self-centered delusions. It is about *Jesus.* The gospel will indeed bring us fame, but it is King Jesus first. Moreover, it is about *his church.* It is a shared fame. We as individuals will enjoy it. But it will be a fame for God's people that depends upon and is inextricably linked to King Jesus's fame.

We already have a sense of how this works. Are you ready to try your hand at Trivial Pursuit? What's common to all these: NSYNC,

Destiny's Child, No Doubt, The Jackson 5, Simon and Garfunkel. Yes, they are all music groups. But more: they are all bands that are best known because of a premier individual performer: Justin Timberlake, Beyoncé, Gwen Stefani, Michael Jackson, Paul Simon.

In fact, once a band dissolves, sometimes it is painfully obvious who had the most talent. After the duo split up, Art Garfunkel's attempt at a solo career flopped while Paul Simon skyrocketed to even greater fame. Yet while all these individual talents were together with their respective bands, the talent and fame of the one was enough to elevate the whole group.

Jesus's honor works similarly. He is the supreme individual human talent. Indeed, Scripture tells us that Jesus, while being human, is the very image of God (the Father) and is in fact a divine person alongside the Father and the Holy Spirit. He is God the Son. He will never leave his church. Through the gospel, the glory that attends him devolves onto us, so that we are dignified. We share his fame.

Two stories follow. Both encourage us to think about how the fame that God wants us to have—*gospel fame*—emerges from a close identification with Jesus. One is ancient, one contemporary.

She Is Gospel Famous

She knew they were trying to murder him. Silently and secretly. No messy public scandal.

He had whipped the crowds into a frenzy with his daring behavior. "Who does he think he is?"—people were saying—"riding down the mountain as a 'king' like that—the very mountain God had designated for his own special purposes in the future?" They said, "He has gone too far."

She had her own opinions.

"What of his outrageous sacrilege in the temple courts?"—they said. Yes, she thought, those animal sellers and money changers work hard to help us worship God. They sell sacrifices and keep the blasphemous coins out of sight. But they work far harder to line their own pockets. She knew Jesus had confronted various authorities in the temple courtyards. She'd even heard rumors that, afterward, Jesus had announced to his disciples that God would soon tear down the whole temple!

They were hell-bent on silencing Jesus. She knew that much. As possible scenes pertaining to Jesus's future filled her mind—bloody and violent—she had to do something. Anything.

They were going to kill him. Not immediately. Once things settled. Passover was just two days away. Jerusalem was teeming. She heard he'd slipped away to nearby Bethany.

When she approached the vendor, he was astonished. She bought pure nard—$50,000 worth—more than a year of wages for the ordinary laborer. Learning that he was in the home of Simon the leper, she found Jesus reclining. She took the alabaster jar, broke the flask, and poured the nard over his head.

As the smell filled the room, mouths flapped open. Most were speechless, but a few vocally upset: "Why was this ointment wasted? It could have been sold and the money used for charity" (Mark 14:4–5, paraphrased).

But Jesus understood. He grasped the heart of the matter immediately—and her own heart too. He knew that she had discerned that his hour had now arrived. Despite his urgent and repeated words, the disciples couldn't see it yet. Somehow she knew. And she wanted to offer all that she could.

"Leave her alone," said Jesus. "Why are you bothering her? She has done a beautiful thing to me" (Mark 14:6, NIV). Jesus reminded his disciples that his time with them would be short. Their opportunity to honor him directly was sand in an hourglass. The poor would always need assistance. "She did what she could," Jesus said, "She poured perfume on my body beforehand to prepare for my burial" (Mark 14:8, NIV).

Then Jesus said something even more striking. Although we don't know her name, this woman is glorious. Honored. She is famous for loving Jesus more than Jesus's clueless and fickle disciples. They jock-eyed for positions of privilege at Jesus's left and right hand. She paid homage to her king. They abandoned him in the night. She prepared him for the pitch-black tomb. They denied even knowing him. She recklessly anointed (messiah-ed or christened) a scandalous targeted man, despite what this would mean for her reputation.

Jesus declared, "Truly I tell you, wherever *the gospel* is pro-claimed throughout the world, *what she has done will also be told, in memory of her*" (Mark 14:9, AT).

The woman with the alabaster jar is *famous* because, by choosing to pay homage in this way, she chose to link her identity to Jesus in an unbreakable fashion. Come what may thereafter, she knew she would be remembered as the woman who chose to honor Jesus in that odd lavish way. She inextricably linked her glory—her fame, honor, and reputation—with Jesus's.

The authorities saw Jesus as a dangerous subversive—worse, a treasonous blasphemer—who deserved to die because he was hated by God. She saw Jesus as the opposite—a man of good news. She had discerned that Jesus was highly regarded by God, and she knew God would highly regard her too if she hitched herself to him.

He was worth her all. By rechristening the Christ, she announced her loyalty to him and his messianic claims—even in his shameful death. This was how she chose to be written into the gospel story. By her actions she entered the "good news" that Jesus was bringing about. *The woman with the alabaster jar is nameless but gospel famous.*

Why Doyle Is Gospel Famous

Doyle Canada. He has a name. Yet he is far less famous than the woman with the alabaster jar. He would probably prefer it that way.

Most of his life was spent in a small logging town, Burney, Cal-ifornia. He married his sweetheart, Sandy, while they were still in high school. They were only seventeen and fifteen, but they couldn't wait. What was there to wait for, anyway? College was for elites in distant cities. The sawmill was right down the road. Life's course was fairly well set for Doyle: work at the mill, pay the bills, buy a house, hunt, fish, camp, party, and raise a few kids.

When we moved to Burney, Doyle was a foreman at the mill. My dad had been hired as the mill's regional forest manager. With a shared love for all things outdoors, they hit it off, and a fast friendship soon joined our families. It seemed every weekend we were in their backyard, or they in ours.

Church? Too busy with life.

When I was in sixth grade, tragedy struck. Doyle had transferred to a new sawmill in a nearby town. When logs went through, an improperly installed piece of machinery occasionally caused pieces of two-by-fours to shoot through irregularly. A jagged splinter shot a hundred feet through the air and lodged midway through Doyle's body, piercing his bowels and spine. He was rushed to the ICU where he languished for weeks. Against desperate odds, eventually Doyle recovered. But he never walked again.

Once we were able to visit Doyle, we expected despondency. His ability to hunt, fish, and horse around—everything he held dear—had been snatched away. We discovered, however, a new man. Transformed. Radiant. A noticeably *more abundant* life. Not that he was never discouraged or stricken with grief. But he was knit together with a different fabric of joy.

In the hospital, Doyle had met Jesus. He believed God had given him a second chance in life—utterly undeserved—and he intended to pursue it in a new Jesus-first fashion. He wheeled into a local church, along with his wife Sandy. His joy was infectious and inviting. Within a month, we were there too.

It was in this church—Grace Community Bible Church—that I would receive baptism, attend youth group, and discover a community of people who genuinely loved our Lord Jesus. Grace is an apt description. Our family was coming under its sweet sway too. Doyle was a man who understood grace.

Doyle died thirteen years ago. After his accident, he still got to hunt and fish plenty. The numerous scenes of Doyle that play through my mind are held together by a common thread: my dad would always pick Doyle up before dawn. I mean *literally* pick him up. He would deadlift Doyle out of his wheelchair into the passenger seat of our truck. Upon arrival Dad would then throw Doyle onto a chair in the Bass Tracker or the duck boat. Then we'd be out on the lake.

The paralysis was challenging. Doyle would have to insert a catheter to pee. Dad would have to help Doyle occasionally and then dispose of the contents. My dad is an active, nonbookish man. Learning to serve Doyle in this practical selfless way was a form of grace for my dad too.

Here is what I want to say about Doyle: he opted to enter into the gospel story, the good news of our Lord Jesus. He saw "the light of *the gospel* of *the glory* of the Christ, who is the image of God" (2 Cor. 4:4, AT). He embraced the gospel and was immersed in its overflowing glory. Because of this Doyle became gospel famous: "Wherever the gospel is preached throughout the world *by me*, what *Doyle* has done will *often* be told, in memory of *him*" (Mark 14:9, personalized).

Doyle is nearly as nameless as the woman with the alabaster jar and far less famous by earthly standards. But his loyalty to Jesus and his testimony mattered to my dad, to our family, and *to me*. And who knows to how many others through secondary and tertiary impact.

Doyle is gospel famous to me. More important, I am confident that he is gospel famous to our Lord Jesus. There are a vast number of people downstream from Doyle's testimony who have been changed. A key gospel purpose is the restoration of God's glory, his fame, and how we come to share in it. Who can guess the "eternal weight of glory" (2 Cor. 4:17, AT), the gospel fame, that will attend Doyle's future in the resurrection age? Because he allowed Jesus to change him, Doyle is famous in and through our Lord Jesus.

The lead singer of Counting Crows, Adam Duritz, got what he wanted but suffered trauma. When fame carried him to the forefront of the music scene, the loneliness was searing. Duritz would sometimes change his lyrics during live performances as a warning. He wanted to issue a red alert to his audiences about the emptiness of fame: "We all wanna be big, big, big, big, big stars, but then we get second thoughts about that" and "when everybody loves you, sometimes that's just about as f***** up as you can be."[6]

Mental health issues came with fame for Duritz—issues that he has publicly described to help others: "You go from a stage in front of 10,000 people to a hotel room on your own every night." Duritz said, "It's a rough situation and it's something we all try to survive. . . . It takes its toll. Fame seems like the most fun thing in the world everyone wants to be popular [sic]. That's what everyone thinks they want but it's a rough ride at times."[7]

Fame on the world's terms didn't make life easy or better in the ways Duritz had anticipated. We all want to be highly regarded. We can pursue a me-first path to fame or make a different choice.

What about you? What are you going to do? You've heard about the woman with the alabaster jar and Doyle Canada. Like them, you've also encountered Jesus. You've been confronted with his person, deeds, claims, and the stigma surrounding him. How are you going to choose to be written into his gospel story?

They became famous not by pursuing a me-style fame—but *indirectly* when they honored the Christ and then found his glory redounding to them. Slowly but surely, God's fame will flood the earth.

I hope you choose to become famous not by chasing the wind, but by trusting that honor will come as a by-product of allegiance to the King. I hope that you'll become famous by acting locally as the King's agent. In so doing you will achieve a virtuous fame that lasts—a shared glory with the King and his people.

Questions for Discussion or Reflection

1. It is said that everyone has fifteen minutes of fame. Describe a time when you were the widely seen center of attention. What did you like and dislike in that moment?

2. How is the English word *glory* used differently in the following statements? "Glory, hallelujah. It's a miracle that Jason is OK!" "I guess Jason is in glory now." "Jason is a bad teammate because he wants all the glory."

3. Where is the boundary line between seeking a good reputation and inappropriately striving for fame?

4. Which of the six malformed gospels do you personally find the most obviously wrongheaded or dangerous? Which make you most uncomfortable? Why?

5. Which of the six malformed gospels do you think is the most common in your larger context (for example, in your nation or region)? Which is most common in your immediate circles (for example, among your friends or in your local church)? Why?

6. The six malformed gospels were identified as misshapen because they all are lacking (some more, some less) four associations that are key to the gospel in Scripture. What were these four associations? Which of the four do you find most often to be missing in cultural appropriations of the gospel today?

7. The most straightforward description of the purpose of the gospel in Scripture is "allegiant obedience" to Jesus the Christ in all nations. What does that mean to you right now? How does it relate to purposes of the gospel that you've previously embraced?

8. The book describes how the woman with the alabaster jar became "gospel famous." What does that mean?

9. Beyond the woman with the alabaster jar, choose another character from the Bible and describe how and why you think that person is gospel famous.

10. The book tells the story of Doyle Canada. Tell about someone who is gospel famous to you personally. How is this person's story woven into the story of King Jesus, so that when you tell the gospel, it is easy to make mention of this person too?

11. Serving Doyle was an important gospel experience for the author's dad. What are some experiences that have impacted your appropriation of the gospel?

12. What steps are you taking in your life currently to enter into the gospel story, so that your personal journey is gospel shaped?

Glory's Two Faces

The last chapter showed that a key purpose of the gospel is to make us famous—although only with and through Jesus—along with his church. Although appealing, this is admittedly vague. What shape does this take? How, practically, does it happen?

But hold on.

Perhaps this God-wants-to-make-us-famous business is dangerous. Even if it contains a grain of truth, isn't such a view problematically *human centered*? Isn't the human tendency to usurp God through pride our basic human error rather than part of the gospel solution?

Surely the real point of the gospel is to enhance *God's glory*. God alone is worthy. If we have anything it is only by his grace. God, not humans, deserves all the credit! Surely the purpose of the gospel is God's glory alone, not ours.

This is a legitimate concern. In Ephesians, Paul blesses God for all the benefits we enjoy in the King in conjunction with the gospel: "And you also were included in the Christ when you heard the message of truth, *the gospel of your salvation*." But note what Paul says next, for it pertains to the gospel's purpose: "And having performed the faith-action, you were marked in him with a seal, the promised Holy Spirit, who is a deposit guaranteeing our inheritance until the redemption of those who are God's possession—*to the praise of his glory*" (Eph. 1:13–14, AT). A foundational gospel purpose in Scripture is indeed that humans give glory to God.

An aim of the gospel is that God be praised for his glory. How God brings about salvation through the gospel—the gift of the Holy Spirit to God's people as a down payment guaranteeing the full payout—appropriately results in praise that enhances God's reputation. The gospel is truly aimed toward God's fame.

Scripture also suggests elsewhere that the gospel is purposed toward God's glory. For example, Paul says that the very reason the Christ became a servant was so that he might fulfill God's promises to his people, in order that "the gentiles might *glorify God* for his mercy" (Rom. 15:9, AT). As part of the gospel, Jesus came to fulfill God's promises, so the nations would appropriately revere and honor God (see Rom. 1:1–5; 15:16–20). Clearly a basic purpose of the gospel is that humans glorify God.

It would be wrongheaded to suggest that the purpose of the gospel is mainly human glory, since it is indisputably true that a final aim beyond that is to glorify God. But perhaps it is a mistake to think that human fame or glory inevitably detracts from God's fame or glory.

What if God's glory is wrapped up with our own, so that we can't entirely have one without the other? Perhaps they are *both* purposes of the gospel, because redeemed human honor is essential to God's fullest glory. We must nuance carefully if we are to appreciate Scripture's complete counsel.

In order to best answer *Why the gospel?*, we must come to appreciate the glory cycle in Scripture. But first, let's allow C. S. Lewis to retrain our theological imagination so we are in a better position to appreciate how God's glory is not threatened by redeemed human glory, but is enhanced by it.

The strangest bus ride that C. S. Lewis ever took introduced him to a spectacular woman. Departing from the shabby grayness of an English street, Lewis was on a bus that rose through overwhelming light. The bus stopped only when it had finally arrived in heaven.

Most of the passengers weren't particularly happy about the unexpected destination. The environs of heaven were beautiful but intimidating. The disgruntled passengers departed from the bus—at least those who were willing to test themselves against the landscape.

So goes the story in Lewis's fictional masterpiece *The Great Divorce*. Lewis is not speculating about the details of our future abode. He is probing what sort of people we need to become right now so as to become suited for life in God's presence.

Lewis opts to disembark in heaven. As Lewis stumbles about, trying to acclimate himself to this painful yet delightful new world, eventually he encounters a creature of such astonishing splendor that it is nigh impossible not to worship her—a radiantly beautiful woman.

In a faint whisper Lewis dares to ask his guide: "She seems to be . . . well, a person of particular importance?"

Her name is Sarah Smith and she hails from Golders Green, a typical London suburb in Lewis's day. The point is that, in terms of human fame, among all possible women she was entirely nondescript during her lifetime—drab and ordinary. Yet Lewis's guide replies: "Aye. She is one of the great ones. Ye have heard that fame in this country and fame on Earth are two quite different things."[1]

Lewis's first lesson is that fame on earth and with God are distinct. This world's fame is stingy and exclusive: if I'm famous and your fame is growing, then yours might eclipse mine, stealing my glory. So apart from God changing our perspective, we seek to build our own personal fame by pushing others down. This world's fame is a scarce commodity that individuals jealously hoard. Those caught up in "Christian" celebrity culture today—the obsession over platform, followers, and influence—should take note of its worldliness and danger.

Meanwhile God-style fame is abundant and overflowing. As he dialogues with his guide, Lewis discovers that fame in heaven comes from helping others become glorious too. Lewis asks, "And who are all these young men and women on each side?" His guide replies, "They are her sons and daughters." Lewis states, "She must have had a very large family, Sir." Then his guide explains the dynamic of heavenly fame:

Every young man or boy that met her became her son—even if it was only the boy that brought the meat to her back door. Every girl that met her was her daughter. . . . Those on whom it [her motherhood] fell went back to their natural parents loving them more. Few men looked on her without becoming, in a certain fashion, her lovers. But it was the kind of love that made them not less true, but truer, to their own wives. . . . Every beast and bird that came near her had its place in her love. In her they became themselves. And now the abundance of life she has in Christ from the Father flows over into them.[2]

Lewis is astonished when he discovers how Sarah Smith became famous with God: by sourcing her life in Christ's glory, her own glory had begun to spill over to others. But Sarah's glorious fame doesn't detract from that of others. It only enhances others' glory— as fame ripples ever outward:

It is like when you throw a stone into a pool, and the concentric waves spread out further and further. Who knows where it will end? Redeemed humanity is still young, it has hardly come to its full strength. But already there is joy enough in the little finger of a great saint such as yonder lady to waken all the dead things of the universe into life.[3]

As we shall see, Lewis's portrayal of Sarah Smith's glory captures several basic scriptural truths.

A key purpose of the gospel is to grant us fame. But it is not a self-centered fame. Nor is it a fame apart from Jesus's kingship. Rather it is sourced in the Christ and overflows for other people so they can become more of whom God wishes them to be. While our glory is being restored in and through the Christ, we fill the pools of many others, replenishing their glory too. This brings honor to God.

Are you ready for some shockingly good news? Contrary to popular belief, in Scripture God is not stingy with his glory. He wants to share it with humans. Indeed, he already has—and wants to do so more and more (for example, John 17:10; 17:22; Rom. 8:30). All of this brings honor not merely to us, but to God as well.

But there is a problem: Human glory has become tarnished, fallen, and bankrupt. God must help humans recover their lost glory. It is through this process that ultimately God is most glorified. How does this work? We need to discover the glory cycle in Scripture.

A fundamental purpose of the gospel is glory's recovery. Paul is not speaking haphazardly when he describes the gospel as "the gospel of *the glory* of the Christ, who is the image of God" (2 Cor. 4:4, AT). Nor is Paul speaking idly when he says that in the King we currently are enjoying "the light of the knowledge of God's *glory* displayed in the face of the Christ" (2 Cor. 4:6, AT). We already share in God's glory through King Jesus. Moreover the glory we are experiencing now will increase in the future (2 Cor. 3:18).

As we'll see, because they are all intertwined, the gospel is purposed toward human fame as well as creation's and God's fame. *When God begins to restore human glory through the gospel, a cycle of glory recovery ensues for all creation—and this simultaneously restores God's own glory.*

Double-Sided Glory

If everyone stopped praising God, would God be any less glorious? This question helps us see the complexity of glory, since glory is bound up with value, worth, honor, and reputation. Our gut instinct is to say No! that it is impossible to detract from God's glory. His glory doesn't depend on us. On the other hand, we correctly sense that if people aren't praising God, then he is not receiving the glory that he deserves, resulting in a deficit of glory. So which is it?

A coin has a heads side and a tails. So also glory. We cannot understand glory for both God and humans in Scripture unless we recognize that its two faces are inextricably bound.

Intrinsic Glory

Intrinsic glory is the value that a person or thing has by its nature or essence entirely independent from public opinion or perception. Each substance—living and nonliving—has a distinct inherent worth, because its properties make it unique in comparison with other substances. Intrinsic glory is the worth that someone or something has because it possesses distinct qualities, even when no one is aware of those qualities.

Consider the substances water and gold. Each has a worth connected to their properties that has nothing to do with personal opinion. No matter where you take the measure—on the earth, moon, or Jupiter—and even if nobody is measuring at all, gold is 19.3 times heavier than water. (Water weighs approximately 8.3 pounds per gallon on earth, but gold 160!) Gold and water are inherently distinct in other ways too: water is liquid at room temperature, but gold is solid; water is a solvent but not gold; solid gold is malleable, but frozen water is brittle.

In other words gold and water have characteristics as *objects* that have nothing to do with subjective or private judgments. Thus intrinsic value can also be called the *objective* side of glory. Because the properties each substance bears make it unique, gold and water have their own intrinsic or objective glory.

Acknowledged Glory

But I'll give you a choice. Do you want a bucket of water or gold? You'd doubtless choose the gold, because we value it more.

Gold has a higher ascribed worth than water. But is this always true? Would gold be worth more if you were stranded for two weeks in the desert? If you were on a space mission to Mars? Someday in our planet's future, an ounce of water may well be worth more than an ounce of gold to the average citizen.

We are aware of the unchanging intrinsic value (glory) of certain things. Water is always more glorious than gold for quenching physical thirst. Yet gold is more glorious for crafting durable goods. Nevertheless, our personal assessment of total worth depends on culture and circumstance. Because the human *subject* is the one who determines how much value something holds for them personally, acknowledged glory can also be called the *subjective* side of glory.

In summary, glory has two faces:

1. *Intrinsic glory* = inherent worth, true value; objective, based on a substance's changeless distinct properties.
2. *Acknowledged glory* = circumstantial worth, perceived value; subjective, ascribed, based on how desirable the changeless distinct properties of a substance are held to be by me or my society.

As we shall discover, both God and humans are described in the Bible as having different but appropriate levels of intrinsic and acknowledged glory.

In order to best answer *Why the gospel?* we must come to appreciate the glory cycle in Scripture.

Introducing the Glory Cycle

Let's begin with an overview of the glory cycle. Then we can explore each step of the process in this chapter and subsequently. The purpose of the gospel is to bring humanity full circle—and beyond. But not just for our own sake. The God of glory has even wider aims.

Figure: The Glory Cycle

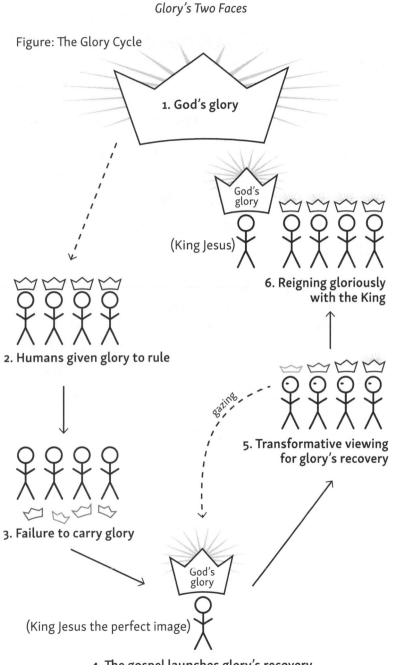

1. God's glory

God's glory

(King Jesus)

6. Reigning gloriously with the King

2. Humans given glory to rule

gazing

5. Transformative viewing for glory's recovery

3. Failure to carry glory

God's glory

(King Jesus the perfect image)

4. The gospel launches glory's recovery

The glory cycle has *six distinct* stages. Since it is vital to this book's argument, please examine the accompanying figure that lists and interrelates each stage carefully. It's important to realize that the glory cycle pertains to humanity as a whole, within epochs of history, but is relevant to each of us personally. Each of us is caught up somewhere in the process.

If the gospel is the good news, then what is the bad? It isn't just Adam and Eve's sin. The bad news is that long ago humanity as a whole lost glory and became stuck in that condition, causing creation and God to lose it too.

But good news! The gospel has launched fame's recovery. As will become clear, in order to recover glory, a perfect *human king* was required—not merely a perfect sacrifice for sins. When the events that constitute the gospel occurred two thousand years ago, *some people* became unstuck—the Jesus-is-King church. Those who have given their allegiance to a new King—those who have declared "faith"— are swinging upward in honor again. Indeed, to such a degree that all creation will encounter God's fame afresh.

Why the gospel? To recovery glory. Humanity's glory and God's glory are interdependent. Because glory is double-sided, involving both intrinsic and acknowledged worth, one can't be fully present without the other. *When God begins to restore human glory through the gospel, a cycle of glory recovery ensues for all creation—and this simultaneously restores God's own glory.*

Yet since a fundamental aim of the gospel pertains to the restoration of the glory that comes from God and returns to him, we must add precision. The foundation of the glory cycle—its starting point—is God's own glory. But as we begin to explore its six stages together, we must seek to answer a clarifying question: How is God's glory bound to his character qualities?

Stage 1: God's Glory

God's intrinsic glory. The glory cycle begins with God's glory. God would have the same undiminished intrinsic glory even if he had never opted to create humans or anything else. God's intrinsic glory can never be diminished or be found lacking.

Scripture speaks often of God's inherent glory—the glory that is essential to God's nature independent of human judgment. For example, when Moses asks to see God's glory, God agrees. Then, we find out why God is worthy as he proclaims the goodness of his divine name, YHWH, revealing his *glory* (see Exod. 33:22).

Consider this episode with care. By God's own self-report, God is revealing his intrinsic glory. If you were to pick out only two words to describe God's self-revelation in this passage, what would you select?

And he passed in front of Moses, proclaiming, "YHWH, YHWH, the compassionate and gracious God, slow to anger, abounding in love and faithfulness, maintaining love to thousands, and forgiving wickedness, rebellion and sin. Yet he does not leave the guilty unpunished; he punishes the children and their children for the sin of the parents to the third and fourth generation." (Exod. 34:6–7, NIV, slightly modified)

What words did you pick?

Since this passage is central to God's self-revelation in the Old Testament, I often ask my college students this question. They most often settle on *loving* and *just*. There are other good answers too. I remind my students that God's desire to show mercy, forgiveness, and loving-kindness is extensive—to the thousands. Meanwhile his punishment of the wicked is real and urgent, but more limited—only reaching to the third and fourth generation.

Through repetition the Hebrew text especially emphasizes God's *hesed*—a difficult word to translate but most often rendered "love." Love in English has strong emotional, psychological, individualistic, and sexual overtones that are not intended in the Hebrew. Whether you *feel* like your heart might burst or whether you are head-over-heels is irrelevant; *hesed* love does not necessarily involve even liking another. *Hesed* is about displayed care: actions that show loyalty, faithfulness to promises, and practical concern for the well-being of others.

What, then, does God's *intrinsic glory* include according to God's own self-revelation in Scripture? At the very least his *covenant love, forgiving nature,* and *justice.* These attributes make God praiseworthy even when humans fail to value or glory in God. God's inherent glory can never lack, decrease, or fade. But, as far as Scripture is concerned, God's intrinsic glory is not the sum total of God's glory, for it has another face.

God's acknowledged glory. God is intrinsically glorious. That is why when God's people are in tune with reality, they can't help but cry out: "Who is he, this King of glory? YHWH Almighty—he is the King of glory" (Ps. 24:10, AT). In fact, those who have encountered God's fame can scarcely do anything other than praise God, summoning all creation to join in the mighty chorus. In a psalm of David we find the refrain, "Be exalted, O God, above the heavens; let your glory be over all the earth"—not once but twice (Ps. 57:5 and 57:11, NIV)! Those who have been caught up in viewing God's honor repeatedly ride the wave of praise as it crashes into the shoreline: "The God of glory thunders, the LORD thunders over the mighty waters" (Ps. 29:3, NIV).

But the Bible also recognizes that humans—individually and within culture—do not value God as we should. This is why God says, "I am YHWH; that is my name! I will not give my glory to another or my praise to idols" (Isa. 42:8, AT). The tension between intrinsic and acknowledged glory is revealed in this passage. God asserts that he has an intrinsic glory or worth, connected to his name YHWH, that the idols entirely lack. But at the same time people are worshipping idols instead of the living God. They are giving the honor that appropriately belongs to YHWH to worthless images. Knowing that this is not in our best interests or the world's, God strenuously objects! He will act to safeguard the acknowledgment of his glory.

Because we do not fully recognize or appreciate God's character qualities, we must be summoned to give God the complete glory he deserves. Scripture calls us again and again to acknowledge God's glory by appreciating his intrinsic glory: "Ascribe to YHWH the glory due his name; worship YHWH in the splendor of his holiness"

(Ps. 29:2, AT; see also 96:8). In this single refrain we see the double-sided nature of glory. The Psalmist affirms that God has a glory that he is owed due to his intrinsic value—the glory due his name. But because we are drawn to worship idols instead, we fail to acknowledge God's infinite worth. So due to human failure, there is a deficit in God's acknowledged glory. If God's fullest glory is to be achieved, humans must be summoned to acknowledge God's worth.

It is not solely humans that should glorify God, rather all creation. The angels are exhorted: "Ascribe to the LORD, you heavenly beings, ascribe to the LORD glory and strength" (Ps. 29:1, NIV).[4] The six-winged seraphim that fly in God's presence cry out: "Holy, holy, holy is the LORD Almighty; the whole earth is full of his glory" (Isa. 6:3, NIV). This reminds us that creation, even its present corrupt state, announces God's fame ceaselessly: "The heavens declare the glory of God; the skies proclaim the work of his hands. Day after day they pour forth speech; night after night they reveal knowledge" (Ps. 19:1–2, NIV). All creation is urged to acknowledge God's glory.

In short, because glory is double-sided, when God's glory is not acknowledged, God experiences an overall glory deficit. God's intrinsic glory can never decrease, but his acknowledged glory has eroded. From a biblical vantage point, acknowledged glory must be optimized for God to receive the maximal glory he deserves. All creation is summoned to appreciate God's intrinsic glory and fame, and to respond by proclaiming it to others. Yet all this is from God. For human and creational glory is sourced in God's glory, fueling the glory cycle.

Stage 2: Humans Given Glory to Rule

Why did God create humans? The Westminster Shorter Catechism captures it with famous pithiness: "Question: *What is the chief end of man?* Answer: *Man's chief end is to glorify God, and to enjoy him forever.*"

You would be hard-pressed to find a Christian, regardless of denomination or tradition, who would fundamentally disagree with what the catechism says about human purpose—myself included. But drawing from Scripture, can we sharpen this?

When we turn to Scripture to discover for what purpose God created humans, it is not first and foremost to glorify God. Something different but related is stressed:

> Then God said, "Let us make mankind in our image, in our likeness, so that they may rule over the fish in the sea and the birds in the sky, over the livestock and all the wild animals, and over all the creatures that move along the ground." So God created mankind in his own image, in the image of God he created them; male and female he created them. God blessed them and said to them, "Be fruitful and increase in number; fill the earth and subdue it. Rule over the fish in the sea and the birds in the sky and over every living creature that moves on the ground." (Gen. 1:26–28, NIV)

Contrary to the catechism, in Scripture the most foundational purpose for which God created humans is *not* to glorify him—at least, not directly. Humans are made for a more specific aim. Notice that *image* and *rule* are mentioned repeatedly in this key passage about human purpose. Meanwhile the concept of image is reinforced by the related term *likeness* and rule by *subdue*. God created humans in his image in order to rule for him.

Although in Scripture God does not create humans for the immediate purpose of glorifying him, nevertheless image and ruling do correlate with glory. *Humans are made in God's image for the purpose of ruling creation on his behalf.* In order to accomplish this task, as part of their image-bearing, God grants humans a derivative glory that is a participation in his intrinsic glory. Although this derivative human glory is sourced in God and comes from him as a gift—so God gets the credit or glory for it—in the end it is not God's glory alone, because he gives it to humans for the sake of creation.

We know this because other passages speak about how God gave humans a share in his glory in order to rule creation. For example, Psalm 8 ponders why the Lord opted to elevate humans:

> What is mankind that you are mindful of them, human beings that you care for them? You have made them a little lower than the angels and crowned them with *glory* (*kabod*) and *honor* (*hadar*). You made them rulers over the works of your hands; you put everything under their feet: all flocks and herds, and the animals of the wild, the birds in the sky, and the fish in the sea, all that swim the paths of the seas. (Ps. 8:4–8, NIV)

God crowned humans with *glory* and *honor* when appointing them *rulers* over creation.

God's glory is present in humans via image-bearing. Moreover, God's glory is made available to other humans and the rest of creation through the dynamic process of humans carrying God's image. For a human to carry the divine image means that God's glory is made present by that human *locally* within creation.

Glory is multiplied through local image-bearing. When creation experiences God's intrinsic glory derivatively through humans who fully bear his image, the result is glory for God, humans, and creation. That is, when a human correctly carries God's image in a local place, that human is honored for serving as a vehicle for God's honor. And when that human in turn points to God as the ultimate source of the goodness, God receives the ultimate acknowledged honor that is his proper due. Proper image-bearing increases glory for humans, creation, and God.

Creation's hunger for God's fame is also why human reproduction is a fundamental human purpose in Genesis—"Be fruitful and multiply and fill the earth and subdue it" (Gen. 1:28, AT). When humans reproduce, more image-bearers are released locally into the world (Gen. 5:3). These image-bearers can then carry God's glory to specific locations within God's creation, satisfying creation's yearning for God's glory.

Human reproduction is necessary if humans are to fulfill their

Proper image-bearing increases glory for humans, creation, and God.

purpose within God's creation project. When humans multiply, the image of God and the capacity for God's glory to be carried to specific locations within creation are also multiplied. This fulfills God's intended purpose for creation.

In sum, each human has a derivative share in God's intrinsic glory as a bearer of God's image. Individual humans were created to flawlessly carry God's image locally, to perfectly reflect God's intrinsic fame in that specific place. This would bring a specific result: that human and God would be made famous—ascribed glory—in a fitting way by other humans and all creation within that location.

Thus, a better (more precise) way to answer the question posed by the Westminster Catechism would be as follows: Question: *What is the chief end of man?* Answer: *God created humans in his image to rule creation on his behalf, so that creation could experience God's glory derivatively through local human rule. The end result is glory for creation, humans, and above all God.*

Perhaps it is now clear why the catechism's statement about human purpose captures truth but needs sharpening. In the catechism's statement, God's glory appears to be a scarce commodity that belongs to him alone. It is one-sided. By implication it is the duty of any and every God-fearing person to safeguard God's glory jealously so that nobody steals it.

But when we use Scripture to enhance precision, we discover that God's glory has two faces—intrinsic and acknowledged. Moreover, we discover that God doesn't jealously hoard his glory, rather he creates humans in such a way that they by nature participate in it. Importantly, rather than keeping all the glory for himself, God wants humans to share in his glory more and more. Since God is its source and final end, the recovery of human glory accelerates the restoration of God's glory.

In sum, a share in God's intrinsic glory is given to humans as part of their image-bearing. Humans must reflect God's *intrinsic* glory in an undiminished fashion if God's *acknowledged* glory is to reach its fullness. God can't receive the fullest glory—worth, value, honor, fame—unless humanity is able to radiate his glory maximally so that as many humans, and as much of creation, as is possible honor him. *God's intrinsic glory can never be diminished, but a full attainment of God's acknowledged glory depends on a maximal recovery of human glory.*

Stage 3: Failure in Carrying Glory

Now the glory cycle takes a dark turn. We all know the story of Adam and Eve's disobedience. Moreover, since we are all "in Adam," a name which in Hebrew simply means human—we must recognize that we have all made the same choice. You and I have eaten from the tree by deciding for ourselves what is good and evil rather than accepting God's wise rule. The result is that we deserve death and punishment for our sins, just as they did.

A basic human problem is that we deserve punishment and death for our sins (Rom. 1:32; 6:23). Each of us personally needs a substitute to cleanse us from sins, so we can be reestablished in a right relationship with God. So, the erasure of our guilt is the basic purpose of the gospel, right? Well, not exactly.

We are so self-absorbed that we have trouble even beginning to think about salvation from a God-centered point of view. Here's the issue: when we assume that the *fundamental* problem—the most foundational bad news—is *our guilt* before God for *our sins*, we are viewing the matter from a selfish perspective. We are putting ourselves—our own individual plight ("I deserve to be punished and die for my sins") and its solution ("I can trust that Jesus is my substitute")—at the center. Don't get me wrong: each of us is personally guilty. We do need rescue so we can be reestablished in our relationship with a holy God.

Less Self-Centered Salvation

But what if we were to think of salvation in a less self-centered way? What if we were to put *God's problem* at the center of salvation rather than ours? And secondarily *creation's problem*?

Imagine God expressing his fundamental dilemma with regard to why his creation project needs rescue—the bad news—this way:

> I designed creation to be ruled by humans. I made them in my image, giving them the ability to reflect my intrinsic honor, because I wanted them freely to choose to make that glory maximally present in every location as they spread over the earth. But humans have opted to dishonor me, creating a glory deficit for me, them, and all creation. Now creation is in a downward spiral, because it is failing to receive the honor it needs. *How can I restore my glory amid humanity, so that creation can experience my glory through human rule as I originally intended?*

In a nutshell, God's salvation problem is this: how can I reestablish my glory (honor) amid humans for their sake, for creation's sake, and for my own sake?

When we see that our *it-is-all-about-human-guilt-and-forgiveness* way of conceptualizing the bad news is self-centered, we are in a better position to discern the gospel's most urgent *why*. Above all, we must recognize this: the bad news is not merely that we deserve death and punishment. It's far worse.

God's whole creation project is threatened by sin, because sin prevents humans from doing what God designed humans to do: to spread his fame to all creation through image-carrying and reproduction. God isn't just trying to erase our guilt. He is trying to undo harm and restore honor. Nor is God's aim to save certain specially chosen humans for heavenly glory while allowing others to be damned so that he can get all the glory exclusively for himself through that process. That is to misunderstand how glory functions within Scripture in God's master story. The glory God is trying to restore is creation's, ours, and his—for they are all mutually dependent and intertwined. This is the problem God is in the process of solving through the gospel.

God's Problem Magnified

When we return to Scripture with a God's-eye perspective on the bad news, we learn more about its severity. Romans 1:18–31 is like a magnifying glass that permits us to see the problem from God's vantage point in detail.

In Romans 1:18, Paul begins his famous description of the human predicament. Once we've been reacclimated to the bad news, we see that the deepest problem is not human guilt per se. Rather human sin causes a glory deficit that jeopardizes all creation.

The problem is loss of glory through a foolish exchange. The wrath of God, Paul explains, is being revealed from heaven because humans have behaved wickedly in suppressing the truth about God (Rom. 1:18). Although God's eternal power and divine nature are self-evident in creation (Rom. 1:19–20)—so that humanity as a whole is without excuse for failing to honor or to thank God (Rom. 1:21)—humans have opted to ignore God.

Why? Because to be human means to eat from the tree of the knowledge of good and evil. We prefer to select what is right and wrong for ourselves—to "claim to be wise" (Rom. 1:22)—rather than to submit to God's revealed wisdom about how humans should behave. We suppress the truth about God because God's behavioral truths are inconvenient for our selfish desires. In our deluded folly we find self-rule preferable to God's rule.

According to Paul, the human choice to become wise in our own eyes resulted not simply in a generic sinfulness, but also in a specific condition: *a loss of glory* due to idolatry. "Although they claimed to be wise, they became fools and *exchanged the glory* of the immortal God for images made to look like a mortal human being and birds and animals and reptiles" (Rom. 1:22–23, NIV). Paul's words echo the description of what happened when the Israelites made the golden calf: "They *exchanged their glory* for the image of an ox that eats grass" (Ps. 106:20, AT). As missionary theologian Jackson Wu puts it, "*God's glory is also their glory.*"[5] So when the Israelites exchanged their glory, that is, God himself, for an idol, the result was a glory loss for themselves too. This glory exchange refers to how idol worship causes a glory failure with regard to our image-carrying.

The Results of the Glory Swap

We are made in the image of God; this is our human dignity. But our human shame is that the glory that attends our image-bearing has been defaced by idolatry. When we worship dehumanizing empty idols—and we've all done this—there is a glory exchange.

Our idolatry leads us to become like the hideous idols we worship (Ps. 115:5–8; 2 Kings 17:5; Jer. 2:5). The lover who worships relational security is consumed by jealousy. The employee who worships money is devoured by greed. The worshiper of moral autonomy bows the knee to tolerance. The final result is a bankruptcy in glory. Yet when we instead worship the one true God—Father, Son, and Holy Spirit—our glory is refreshed and recharged. Greg Beale pithily describes the situation: "We become what we worship."[6]

Although it is often missed by readers of Scripture today, Paul announces that glory loss is the foundational problem solved by the gospel. When, after three chapters detailing the human plight, Paul summarizes, he indicates that the basic problem is sin's relationship to glory loss. Unfortunately, we've acted like Paul's real concern is something else.

Paul's summary is blunt: "All have sinned *and are lacking the glory of God*" (Rom. 3:23, AT). First, let's notice what Paul does *not* say, even though he tends to be misread on this point. Paul does not say, "All have sinned and fall short of God's perfect standard for holiness," nor does he say, "All have sinned and fall short of God's just requirements of the law." Humans do need rescue because they fall short of God's perfect moral standard and his just requirements, but that isn't Paul's precise point here. Paul keeps a God's-eye view of the salvation problem, seeing how sin is disrupting God's plans for creation.

Paul is lamenting humanity's *glory* failure. In other words, the problem with sin is not sin in and of itself—as if the erasure of it and our guilt is the final endgame of salvation. Rather the primary problem with sin is that it is causing a glory deficit. Paul highlights how our sin is bound up with how we "are lacking of the glory of God" because he wants to stress something specific: *how humans are falling short in their image-bearing vocation.*

Humans have worshiped idols rather than God, becoming devoid of God's glory. Sin prevents humans from doing what God needs them to do within creation. Human dishonor has resulted in dishonor for all creation—and because of this God has also been dishonored. As Paul puts it, "You who are boasting in the law are *dishonoring* God through transgressing the law. For, it is written, 'The name of God is blasphemed among the nations because of you'" (Rom. 2:23–24, AT). That is, even God's special chosen people have fallen into the trap of idolatry and disobedience (see 2:18–22), causing God's name to be slandered by all nations. As human glory has declined, God's glory or reputation has diminished too.

In sum, what is the bad news? Our failure to make God's glory present through our image-carrying leads to lost glory for God, humans, and creation. What is the gospel? Paul describes it as "the gospel of the glory of the Christ, who is the image of God" (2 Cor. 4:4, AT). The gospel is that by fully bearing God's glorious image, King Jesus has initialized glory's recovery.

QUESTIONS FOR DISCUSSION OR REFLECTION

1. Describe a time when you took the credit (at least in your own mind if not publicly) rather than giving appropriate honor to others who supported or assisted you.

2. Consider three of your top successes or achievements in the last ten years. How have you honored God for these? Practically speaking, has this honoring enhanced God's reputation in the world? Why is it easy for us to fail to give God the glory (reputation) he deserves?

3. C. S. Lewis's description of a bus ride to heaven is purposed toward helping us consider our flaws in character and virtue. Describe two flaws that are ill-suited for the eternal quality of life that God wants to develop in you. What practical steps can you take to improve?

4. Why is Lewis awed by Sarah Smith? Tell about a person in your life who reminds you of Sarah Smith.

5. Describe a celebrity whom you'd especially like to meet. Is celebrity culture always bad? How should we respond to the tendency to regard certain Christian pastors, musicians, and authors as celebrities?

6. From within a biblical framework, why does God's full glory depend on us?

7. Consider an avocado and a rose. Describe the *intrinsic glory* of each. What is the *acknowledged glory* among your friends? For you personally?

8. List seven qualities or attributes of God that most readily come to mind. Which are intrinsic and which ascribed? Which do you personally value the most? Which do you need to appreciate more?

9. What does the Bible say about the purpose for which humans were made? How does this relate to glory?

10. A popular slogan is *soli Deo gloria* ("glory to God alone").

From a scriptural standpoint, why might a person say this slogan is true but confusing or misleading if not qualified?

11. What is a less self-preoccupied way to describe why salvation is necessary? Why might this reframing be important for the church's ongoing evangelism and mission?

12. Describe one area in your life where you have made the "glory exchange" by worshipping an empty idol. What harm occurred? How was the opportunity to spread God's glory lost?

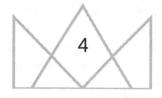

Gospel Recovery

The *why* of the gospel can best be answered by saying that God has given us what we need most—*a king*. But secondarily, why we need a rescuing king—and how that benefits us—is most fully explained by Scripture's glory cycle.

The previous chapter focused on stages 1–3 of the cycle (for an overview of the whole cycle, see p. 57). Humans are made in God's image to govern creation on God's behalf by carrying his glory to creation. When humans cease to worship the living God and instead worship bankrupt idols—money, power, sex, tolerance, and diversity—there is a disruption in glory. Humans and creation cease to function right. God's intrinsic glory is irreducible and unimpeachable. But God's ascribed glory is lacking because humans are not acknowledging God's full worth. The result is a glory deficit for God, humans, and all creation.

Humans have a purpose. A knife is designed to cut; shoes are for footwear. You can use a knife as a soup ladle and a shoe for a coffee pot, but the results will be poor. Given that creation requires correct image-bearing to run properly, when Adam and Eve—representing all humans—rejected God's plan, creation was bound to decay.

Given creation's inevitable corruption, what were God's options? He could have abandoned his entire creation project. Or he could have forsaken his human creatures. But were these really possible for God within the boundaries of his self-giving love if there was another way?

That God chose to clothe Adam and Eve's naked human guilt with garments of skin tells us much about God's commitment to be *for us*. Later God opted to make unbreakable promises to bless all nations through Abraham's offspring and through David's (Gen. 12:3; 22:18; 2 Sam. 7:12–14; Luke 1:32–33; Gal. 3:16).

This chapter is the centerpiece of this book, because it focuses on stage 4 in the glory cycle: *how the gospel initiates glory's recovery*. We will explore what God has already done in history to begin to restore glory. For saving grace is primarily about the free gift that humanity as a whole did not deserve, but which God opted to give *at a specific time in past history*—the events that together constitute the gospel (Acts 14:3; 20:24, 32; Gal. 1:6; Col. 1:6). In the next chapter we will look at how the purpose of the gospel impinges on individuals—you, me, or your unsaved coworker—so each can participate today. The gospel is transformative.

Stage 4: The Gospel Initiates Glory's Recovery

In *Gospel Allegiance* (and *The Gospel Precisely*) I present a ten-part outline of the gospel's content, showing how each event is said to be part of the gospel multiple times in Scripture.[1] I've included it on the right side of the following table for reference, because here I want to go beyond these previous studies by showing that we can detect three basic theological movements within the gospel's content. These three theological movements connect to the gospel's *why*. To make that clear I've added a framing sentence that speaks of King Jesus's role in restoring glory.

The gospel is that God is in the process of restoring glory through Jesus the rescuing King, who:

1. Incarnation
1. preexisted as God the Son,
2. was sent by the Father,
3. took on human flesh in fulfillment of God's promises to David,

2. Death for Sins
4. died for our sins in accordance with the Scriptures,
5. was buried,

3. Raised to Reign
6. was raised on the third day in accordance with the Scriptures,
7. appeared to many witnesses,
8. *is enthroned at the right hand of God as the ruling Christ,*
9. has sent the Holy Spirit to his people to effect his rule, and
10. will come again as final judge to rule.

When we delve into the theology of Jesus's incarnation, death for sins, and resurrection to kingship, we are unearthing the *why* of the gospel foundationally. Because creation needs humans to rule per God's design, the gospel starts with the gift of a human who is born to reign flawlessly. The gospel begins with the King's enfleshment.

1. Incarnation

It is one of the most famous verses in the Bible. Perhaps you've even memorized it. But if the word *glory* to you has previously been vague and disconnected from God's overarching plan, perhaps you've never caught why it is gospel: "The Word became flesh and made his dwelling among us. We have seen his *glory*, the *glory* of the one and only Son, who came from the Father, full of grace and truth" (John 1:14, NIV).

Incarnation means entering into human flesh. God the Son is eternal along with the Father and the Spirit. The Son preexisted alongside God the Father and was active in creating the world. But while continuing to be fully God, the Son opted to take on our complete humanity at a specific moment in the first century.

The incarnation is foundational to the gospel because the problem that God is trying to correct is a lack of his *glory* amid creation—a deficit that exists because humans are not carrying God's glory to it in their image-bearing.

The true gospel doesn't reject Israel's law or its story; rather the gospel fulfills God's intentions for his people. Israel was to carry God's glory to the nations but failed to do so perfectly. So God acted to fulfill Israel's calling by sending the Son to take on human flesh in the person of Jesus. "Jesus adopts the vocation of the people of God as the bearers of Yahweh's name," as Carmen Joy Imes puts it.[2] When the Son takes on human flesh, flawlessly bearing God's image, then bankrupt humanity suddenly has an opportunity to view God's unimpeded glory. Now a human, Jesus, is doing precisely what God designed all humans to do.

The Glory Blazes Forth

In his incarnation, the Son begins to blaze forth God's glory to all other humans and the rest of creation, so God's fame can be experienced through him. King Jesus is *the paradigm for humanity*. In fact, Jesus's favorite title for himself, the Son of Man, means the person that best represents the category "human." Yet the title also was associated with attainment of royal rule at the right hand of God (for example, Ps. 80:17; Dan. 7:13–14; Matt. 26:64). Jesus both *is* and *represents* optimal humanity.

The apostle Paul also makes it clear that the incarnation is where the gospel begins. Paul's most famous letter, Romans, opens with a description of the gospel. Paul calls it "the gospel of God," indicating that God "promised it in advance" in Scripture (Rom. 1:1–2, AT).

Paul further describes this gospel by saying that it is about God's Son, who "came into being" by means of the seed of David (Rom. 1:3, AT). This refers to how the Son preexisted, but also became human by means of Mary, who was from the family of David.

In Paul's description of the gospel, we know the incarnation is in view because Paul says this "coming into being" was not a coming into existence in every sense. This "coming into being" was only "as it pertains to the flesh" (Rom. 1:3, AT). The enfleshment of the Son is the good news that begins glory's recovery.

As Paul makes clear, the incarnation was not an end unto itself—it led to other events identified as part of the gospel: Jesus's resurrection and his installation as "Son-of-God-in-Power" (Rom. 1:4, AT). That is, the incarnation was aimed toward the most basic gospel purpose: Jesus's enthronement in the ultimate position of cosmic power—so all nations could yield "allegiant obedience" to him (Rom. 1:5, AT).

The Incarnation's Royal Trajectory

Mysteriously, even prior to creation God had already determined to make a special people for himself in and through a king. The apostle Paul details this mystery: God "chose us in the Christ before the creation of the world to be holy and blameless in his presence" (Eph. 1:4, AT). The Christ, the future King, was in view *even prior to creation*.

Elsewhere Paul explains how the future king could be a preexistent pattern. He calls Adam "a type of the one to come" (Rom. 5:14, AT). We might have expected Paul to say that Adam was the original human and the King became human later to rescue creation. Strange as it may seem, that is not how it works. The future ideal king—"the one to come"—is the human prototype on the basis of which God crafted Adam. Adam appeared first in time, but Adam was crafted in anticipation of the model human—the king!—who would arrive in the future.

The preexistent king, now enfleshed as Jesus, is the original human while Adam is the inferior copy. It is as if God sent a model rocket into the world first and then announced that the model rocket was actually based on a fantastic, already designed NASA spaceship that he would send in the future. Adam's creation was based on the ideal human king that God would one day send.

Incarnation Regardless

In saying such things, Scripture indicates that even if Adam and Eve had not sinned, the incarnation would have happened anyway. Prior to the fall, the triune God—Father, Son, and Spirit—already intended to send the Son to take on human flesh to rule creation as the ideal King.

God had planned for the development and spread of human civilization prior to the fall. Remember, the human mandate to multiply, fill the earth, subdue it, and rule over it is given *prior to* Adam and Eve's disobedience. Accordingly, humanity and creation began in an immature state in the garden. But God intended progress toward a city, the new Jerusalem.

The fall tragically tainted the developmental process. But even had the fall never happened, the incarnation would have occurred regardless—the gift of the ultimate King—in order to bring creation to the maturity that God intends for it. Because they are prior to the fall within Scripture's overarching story, incarnation and kingship are more foundational to the gospel—more basic to it—than the cross and resurrection. However, in light of Adam and Eve's disobedience, the incarnation became a rescue operation too. Then the cross and resurrection became essential to the gospel also.

2. Death For Sins

The incarnation shows us that salvation is not just *from* but also *for*. When we fail to see that the incarnation is every bit as much gospel as the cross, we misunderstand and limit the cross. When considered in isolation, it is easy to treat the cross as if it is exclusively about salvation *from* guilt, sin, and death. It truly is about those things. But when we follow Scripture's lead by starting the gospel with the incarnation, we see why the gospel's framework is royal. The incarnation teaches us that the cross is also *for* the recovery of glory, since it expresses and leads to perfect human rule. Salvation is not just rescue *from* negative consequences, but is rescue *for* restoration to full health.

Yet we dare not neglect the cross. Because they would have occurred regardless of the fall, the incarnation and the coming of the Christ-King may be more foundational to the gospel than the cross, but that is not to say the cross is less important or less essential to it. God forbid! Jesus's accomplished work on the cross for us is a bedrock gospel purpose.

Scripture gives us several images to help us grasp why Jesus's death is good news. Scholars call these *models of atonement*. As Joshua McNall reminds us, it is best to see these models not as competitors, but as contributors to a larger portrait.[3] Only when held together, next to one another, can we appreciate how each contributes something essential to the whole message of how the cross saves.

Consider the four following models of the atonement as tools to help us better understand God's purposes in giving the gospel.

(1) Substitution

Substitution involves one person or thing replacing another. At the heart of substitutionary atonement is a simple but profound biblical truth: the King died on the cross in our place for our sins. But there are various subtheories—ransom, penal, governmental, satisfaction—that seek to nuance and adorn this simple truth. These subtheories are helpful, but aspects of each have also attracted controversy.

Substitution is part of the gospel. When the apostle Paul outlines the gospel, he declares that the Christ "died *for* [*hyper*] our sins"

(1 Cor. 15:3). The Greek word *hyper* usually involves substitution, so that we could equally translate: the Christ died "in behalf of our sins" or "for the sake of our sins" (see Gal. 1:4). But to understand substitution, we need to appreciate various metaphors in Scripture that fill out its meaning.

The Ransom Theory

Jesus himself speaks about substitutionary atonement: "For even the Son of Man did not come to be served, but to serve, and to give his life as a *ransom* for many" (Mark 10:45, NIV). The Greek word *lutron* (ransom) refers to the price necessary to release prisoners of war or those in debt-bondage.[4]

Substitution is in view because Jesus offers himself in place of others. Jesus encourages us to picture his life as enormously valuable, so it can be used to purchase a great many lives. In giving his life, Jesus himself is the one who takes the "loss" in order to make the payment that will free others.

The ransom theory of atonement is indisputably biblical. But what are its limits? For example, if we follow the metaphor, to whom is payment made? To the Father? To Satan?

Some early church fathers, like Origen, were convinced that Jesus had to pay the devil: "Now it was the devil who was holding us, to whom we had been dragged off by our sins. Therefore he demanded the blood of Christ as the price for us."[5] For Origen, the devil refused to release his captives until he received the hard currency of the Christ's blood. Others, like Cyprian, were persuaded that Jesus on the cross was like a baited trap. When Satan took the bait, Jesus became our substitute: we were snatched from "the jaws of the devil" and ransom was offered to the Father.[6] In this way, Jesus was felt to have deceived the deceiver.

But payment to Satan is unlikely. Many ancient and nearly all contemporary theologians—rightly in my judgment—find a ransom payment to the devil highly problematic. For example, since the one God—Father, Son, and Holy Spirit—is properly sovereign and Satan is a deceitful usurper, it is false to assume that Satan has legal right to payment. Neither Jesus nor the Father *owe* Satan anything.

It is best to affirm that in offering his life in place of others, Jesus releases a mighty host of prisoners, and to leave the question of who is owed the ransom unanswered. After all, Jesus didn't feel a need to spell out an answer for his audience. Our theories of atonement are in the end metaphors that point to theological realities. But such metaphors neither exhaust nor uniformly map onto those realities.

The best response to the ransom metaphor is to silence our speculation and then to worshipfully celebrate its basic truth: the Son gave his life to release us from bondage.

Penal Substitutionary Atonement

The person who makes the ransom payment suffers a "financial" loss to release those held captive. So the ransom metaphor suggests that by voluntarily suffering unto death so that his life could serve as a payment, Jesus was accepting a loss or penalty to redeem others. Jesus's voluntary acceptance of a liability or penalty by standing in place of others as part of an official transaction has come to be called *penal substitutionary atonement.*

However, theologians who use the full phrase *penal substitutionary atonement* can mean quite different things by each of those three words. This makes any conversation about it fraught.

The term *penal* is especially slippery. For example, does penal refer to any loss, suffering, or penalty in general? Or does there need to be an official legal transaction for it to count as penal? If so, what precisely is transacted, what parties are involved, does the attitude in which the transaction is conducted matter for its efficacy, what code of law is in view, and what are the results for each party and the world? For these reasons and more, it is unwise either to affirm or disavow *penal* substitutionary atonement without giving an exact definition.

To define *penal* and defend that definition is beyond this book's reasonable scope. But we can undertake, briefly, what I would consider the more important task: to appreciate pertinent imagery from Scripture regardless. We've already discussed ransom. Additionally let's briefly consider a few powerful images in Scripture that must be taken into account by anyone working on this topic.

The apostle Peter reflects on Jesus as the suffering servant announced by Isaiah. This servant is described by Isaiah in graphic terms: "he was pierced for our transgressions, he was crushed for our iniquities; the punishment that brought us peace was on him, and by his wounds we are healed" (Isa. 53:5, NIV) and "for the transgression of my people he was struck" (Isa. 53:8, AT). Peter quotes Isaiah to show that on the cross Jesus carried our sins upon his body: "'He himself bore our sins' in his body on the cross, so that we might die to sins and live for righteousness; 'by his wounds you have been healed" (1 Pet. 2:24, AT). The servant serves as a proxy for the people to heal them, suffering wounds in his body for their violation of God's ways (see 1 Pet. 3:18).

In a similar way the apostle Paul presents the Son as a substitute who carries human sin and experiences its consequences. For example, consider Paul's claim that God did what the law could not do "by sending his own Son in the likeness of sinful flesh concerning sin [*peri hamartias*]" (Rom. 8:3, AT). Substitution is involved because his being "in the *likeness* of sinful flesh" requires that although Jesus himself was not sinful, Jesus had in some way become akin to sinful flesh by standing in our place.

The Son became like sinful flesh while remaining sinless by carrying our sin. King Jesus did this so we could become righteous in God's eyes, but at the same time God's justice would be upheld (see 2 Cor. 5:21). Paul's logic works this way: God's righteousness requires that he bring judging wrath against sin (Rom. 1:17–18; 2:5; 3:5). Humans create sin, so even though it becomes a cosmic monster that they can't control, they are guilty for it and justly deserve punishment—which is death (Rom. 1:32; 6:23).

Yet God was motivated by his boundless love for us even in the midst of our guilt. So he acted: "God demonstrates his own *love for us* in this: While we were still sinners, the Christ died *for us*"

The Son became like sinful flesh while remaining sinless by carrying our sin.

(Rom. 5:8, NIV slightly modified). Don't miss what is at the heart of what has traditionally been called penal substitutionary atonement: *God's love. For us.*

Motivated by love, the Son took sin upon his flesh, bearing the death penalty that we deserve. So through the crucifixion, God "condemned sin in the flesh" (Rom. 8:3, AT). That is, God rendered a decisive verdict against sin as it was carried in Jesus's flesh on the cross. This means the King suffered in our place to set us free, so that the law's just requirement might be fully met in us (Rom. 8:4). In summary, when sin was condemned in his flesh, the sinless Son was a substitute carrying our human sin in his flesh, bearing the penalty for sin and death that we justly deserved. To receive this cleansing freedom, a human must enter the Spirit-filled community. Then they are led by the Spirit rather than the flesh (Rom. 8:5–14).

The Cross's Work within Enthronement

Even though Jesus said, "it is finished" (John 19:30), the work of the cross was not fully effective for us until after Jesus's resurrection and heavenly installation. Jesus was put forward by God as the *hilasterion*, the mercy seat—the lid of the ark of the covenant where purifying blood was sprinkled each year by the high priest (Rom. 3:25; see also Lev. 16:14–15). When the resurrected Jesus ascended bodily to the right hand of God, then he became not only King but also our priestly intercessor (Rom. 8:34), making atonement in God's heavenly presence. As theologian Patrick Schreiner reminds us, the ascension "not only confirmed Christ's work, but contributed to and even continues Christ's work."[7]

After his resurrection, the Son, in his capacity as High Priest, made a once-for-all-time presentation of his own purifying blood in the heavenly realm (Heb. 9:11–12). In and through the King, the high priestly offering of this blood cleanses humans past, present, and future from sin so that they have right standing with God, but at the same time it maintains God's just punishment of sin (Rom. 3:25–26).

The result of this atoning work? In the King, humans are no longer liable for God's just wrath against sin, but are instead reconciled to God (Rom. 5:9–10). The work of the cross for us was not finished until Jesus ascended to be enthroned as King and High Priest.[8] After attaining the cosmic throne, King Jesus's saving benefits become available to God's people through his reign, intercession, and the sending of the Spirit. This is why the gospel, and our response to it, must be king first.

Qualifying Penal

I've already indicated that some reject *penal* substitutionary atonement because the term is ambivalent. In my judgment, this is fine as long as we aren't simultaneously denying Scripture's imagery outlined above. Yet others reject penal for a different but clearly false reason: they feel the word *penal* implies that God undertakes violent revenge by allowing his wrath to fall on the Son. Or that God the Father is implicated in child abandonment. They conclude that the God of penal substitutionary atonement is immoral and substandard, and therefore the doctrine is necessarily false. But to draw such implications is wrongheaded.

To suggest that *penal* necessarily implies a violent, vengeful, abandoning God is merely to caricature. Such caricatures misunderstand the true relationship between Father, Son, and Holy Spirit. Our theories of atonement can't suggest a fracture in intra-Trinitarian life. We cannot pit one person of the Trinity against the others—as if the Son doesn't wish to bear our penalty but is forced to do so by a petty, abusive Father. Moreover, the idea that the Father abandoned the Son on the cross is contrary to Scripture. Jesus's words to his disciples in the garden directly oppose such a view: "A time is coming and in fact has come when you will be scattered, each to your own home. *You will leave me all alone. Yet I am not alone, for my Father is with me*" (John 16:30, NIV). Jesus knew that even though his disciples would abandon him during his passion and crucifixion, the Father would remain with him always.

On the cross the Son *felt* abandoned. He expressed his agony with words from Psalm 22:1: "My God, my God, why have you forsaken me." But we know our human feelings do not always represent reality. Beyond his temporary feelings, Jesus knew that God does not forsake the righteous person who loyally trusts. Jesus had prophesied at least three times that he would be killed *and then raised from the dead* (for example, Mark 8:31; 9:31; 10:34). The Father would hear his outcry and deliver him—as the rest of the Psalm 22 makes clear (verses 4–5, 21–31). The willing sacrifice of the Son's body in anticipation of his exaltation was the triune God's plan even before the moment of Jesus's incarnation (John 17:4–5; see also Heb. 10:5–7). Jesus knew the Father had not truly forsaken him.

Regardless of whether the term *penal* is preferred or not, here is the theological bottom line: God the Father loves us even though—because he is inalterably just—he must pour out his wrath against sin as an act of justice. The Son, since he is fully God too, has the exact same standard of justice and love as the Father—as does the Spirit. Because the Father, eternal Son, and Spirit are all one—and their actions directed toward the created order are ultimately inseparable—on the deepest theological level, it is not the Father's wrath alone that is justly poured out against human sin, but the eternal Son's and the Spirit's wrath too. The persons of the Trinity work together for our salvation by allowing Jesus the Son to carry our sins as a substitute.

The Governmental Theory

A king represents his people. While recognizing the strength of substitutionary atonement—with many preferring to add penal too—some find that Scripture allows a further nuance. The governmental theory is a form of penal substitutionary atonement, but it limits the amount of suffering involved for Jesus.

In the governmental theory of atonement, the penalty Jesus suffers is comparable to how a senator represents his constituents. The governmental theory suggests that Jesus did not bear the exact penalty for every single sin committed, contending that would be an unfathomable amount of sin and would require more than Jesus's brief suffering. Rather as the head of humanity, Jesus bore *a lesser representative but sufficient penalty* that was commensurate with what his people deserved, but not the exact penalty. For governmentalists, God showed that he upholds the moral order of the universe for all humans in this way.

The Satisfaction Theory

Penal substitution is closely related to the satisfaction theory of atonement. The satisfaction theory—most closely associated with the medieval theologian Anselm—proposes that God is *offended* by human sins, so a fitting reparation must be made by humans to clear the dishonoring offense.

Sin brings God into disrepute. It calls into question his goodness, justice, and honor among the nations. Within the satisfaction theory, only a human so perfect that he is in fact fully divine is able to satisfy a perfect God by restoring his honor. Although it is not strictly necessary that the mechanism by which satisfaction is offered involve penal substitution, it is common today to blend these theories of the atonement.

As we reflect on the various possible nuances of substitutionary atonement, the upshot is this: no matter what model is advanced, we must bear in mind that the Son voluntarily took on human flesh, truly suffered in his human nature as he died for our sins, and willingly served as a sacrifice (see Heb. 10:5–10). In so doing he offered each of us the opportunity to be reconciled to the triune God. Father, Son, and Spirit are on the same team for our salvation.

Moreover, substitutionary atonement also shows that although its full extent was long hidden, the purpose behind all other gospel purposes is simply this: God's extraordinary love. The cross unveils the astonishing height, depth, and breadth of God's love. Not only do Father, Son, and Spirit love us despite our sins, God loves us so much that the Son was willing to suffer in that unbelievably cruel way for us.

Why the gospel? *Beyond all else, the gospel is motivated by God's cross-shaped, self-emptying love for us.*

(2) Victorious Kingship

A second model of the atonement features victorious kingship. Although substitution is what is most readily associated with the cross in popular Christian imagination, the Bible gives front billing to a different image: *Christus Victor*! This Latin phrase means "The messiah is the conqueror!"

Christus Victor!

Christus Victor is the dominant image for atonement in the New Testament, because the picture of Jesus as the victorious King is invoked every time the term *Christ* is applied to the resurrected and enthroned Jesus. Victory is the larger category; substitution is a subset within it. Although both are prominent and essential, *Jesus's identity as the triumphant Christ* is emphasized far more in the New Testament than Jesus as our substitute. Meanwhile the cross was the primary means by which the King won the victory.

Jesus conquered his enemies on the cross, resulting in his kingship. Although this involved substitutionary purification with respect to human sins, the cross's victory goes beyond substitution. Jesus's death, for example, did not substitute for or otherwise purge the sins of demons, evil spirits, or Satan, but nevertheless it defeated them. Paul puts it this way, "And having disarmed the powers and authorities, he [the Christ] made a public spectacle of them, triumphing over them by the cross" (Col. 2:15, NIV).

The True Enemies

Although Jesus was put to death by wicked men, they were not Jesus's ultimate enemies. Humans are culpable for their sins. But human wickedness is empowered by even more sinister forces—Satan and his minions. These are Jesus's more basic enemies, because they inspire the wicked earthly regimes and broken systems that ensnare humans. This is what Paul means by "the powers and authorities" (Col. 2:15; see also Eph. 6:12). The cross disarmed these foes. But even in their defeat, these evil spiritual powers are permitted to rage on temporarily. Paul can say "many live as enemies of the cross of the Christ" (Phil. 3:18), because these forces continue to empower human wickedness. This is why evil still abounds in the world despite Jesus's kingship.

Yet when God deems the time ripe, "the end will come," at which time the Messiah will hand "over the kingdom to God the Father, after he has destroyed all dominion, authority and power" (1 Cor. 15:24, NIV). That is, these evil spiritual powers have already been defeated, but in the end their authority will be utterly abolished.

Victorious Rule

Meanwhile, the resurrected Christ is seated above these evil spiritual forces. The Messiah is at God's right hand "far above all rule and authority, power and dominion, and every name that is invoked, not only in the present age but also in the one to come" (Eph. 1:21, NIV). From that exalted position he is ruling victoriously until all his enemies are subdued: "For he must reign until he has put all his enemies under his feet" (1 Cor. 15:25, NIV).

"The last enemy to be destroyed is death" (1 Cor. 15:26, NIV). Like evil spiritual powers, the final enemy—death—has been conquered by the victorious Christ already but has not yet been destroyed. Finally King Jesus will eradicate even death. Then, Paul says, all things except the Father will be subject to the King of kings and the Lord of lords (1 Cor. 15:27–28).

(3) Moral Influence

The moral influence theory of atonement contends that Jesus's death rescues us by showing us a pattern that proves to be saving when we adopt it. Yet because Jesus's death involved intentionality, his death's significance is informed by his life and teachings. Therefore, to be saved we must learn how to behave from Jesus's holistic moral example. *That is, in order to enter salvation, we must become disciples of Jesus.*

Discipleship Is Saving

To enter salvation and arrive at its final goal we must choose to follow and apply the Master's way of life and teachings. God's atoning rescue happens as we undertake the life-unto-death-unto-new-life pattern that Jesus exemplified.

The biblical underpinnings for the moral influence theory of atonement are firm. For example, Jesus says: "Whoever wants to be my disciple must deny themselves and take up their cross and follow me. For whoever wants to save their life will lose it, but whoever loses their life for me and for the gospel will save it" (Mark 8:33–34, NIV).

Following Jesus's behavioral example is not optional for rescue from our sinful condition. Jesus says that it is essential that we undertake a cross-shaped life of discipleship to be saved. We must be loyal to Jesus and his way of life. Moreover, Jesus makes it clear in context that he is speaking of final or ultimate salvation, not temporary rescue. What is at stake is one's essential self (*psychē*, traditionally translated "soul") and personal vindication when Jesus returns to render final judgment (Mark 8:36–38).

When queried by his disciples, "Lord, are only a few people going to be saved?" Jesus did not say, "Yep, only the few who trusted exclusively in my death for sins." Rather, Jesus says, "Make every effort to enter through the narrow door" (Luke 13:23–24, NIV). Jesus calls his followers to strive to imitate his manner of life. He warns that on the day of the great kingdom feast, many will claim to know him, but since they are in practice "evildoers," Jesus will disown them (Luke 13:26–27; see also Matt. 7:13–27 esp. verse 23). They will be cast away from Jesus's kingdom banquet (Luke 13:28).

The genuineness of discipleship is revealed through action. With regard to the cold, sick, stranger, imprisoned, and naked, on the day of judgment Jesus will say, "Whatever you *did* for one of the least of these brothers of mine, you *did* for me" (Matt. 25:40, AT). On the basis of this *doing*, Jesus will accordingly issue a verdict for or against us, separating the sheep and the goats (Matt. 25:31–46).

Final salvation depends on imperfect but authentic discipleship. We must learn from King Jesus so that our faith extends into obedient doing. We are saved by allegiance to the King since allegiance unites us to the King and his benefits.

Personal Justification First?

Despite Jesus's words about the necessity of discipleship into his life-pattern for final salvation, some suggest that moral influence is less foundational than personal justification by faith. They argue that first we need to experience God's regenerating power so we can express faith in Christ and be personally justified (declared righteous)—and only afterward can we successfully come under the tutelage of Jesus's moral influence by submitting to his lordship. They contend that if we try to submit to Jesus as King before trusting him as Savior, we fall into the death trap of attempting self-salvation through our own moral efforts.

In other words, some say that we have to have faith in Christ's accomplished work on the cross as Savior first, and only subsequently can we attempt to submit to him as King. But as Scripture presents the matter, this is 100 percent backward. It misunderstands what "faith" means (*pistis*) and how it relates to the Christ as part

89

of the gospel. There is no salvation apart from Jesus's kingship, for it only comes through his kingship.

Justified by Moral Influence

We are not justified apart from Jesus's moral influence but rather through it. Jesus's moral influence is exerted over us through the process by which he came to be enthroned as the Christ, affecting what it means to have faith as we seek justification. There is no king for us to have "faith in" with respect to the gospel that can be separated from Jesus's moral choices that led to his kingship.

Moral influence is as foundational as substitutionary atonement because through loyalty Jesus was justified and became the Christ. He did this so we could become loyal to him as the Christ and could be justified too. Jesus's own justification by his faith, or loyalty (*pistis*), comes before ours and is purposed toward causing ours. As Paul states, "in the gospel the righteousness of God is revealed by *pistis* for *pistis*, just as it is written, 'The righteous one by *pistis* will live'" (Rom. 1:17, AT). The *pistis* of the Christ stimulates our human *pistis* toward the Christ (Rom. 3:21–22; Gal. 2:16; 3:22). That is, in the gospel, justification is revealed by the King's *pistis* (*faith* or *loyalty*) for the purpose of stimulating our *pistis* (*faith* or *loyalty*), resulting in life. Jesus is the righteous one who by faith lives, becoming the Christ. When we declare faith in him as the Christ, we are righteous and live too.

Let me show why Jesus' moral influence over us is foundational to our personal justification by faith by attempting to lay bare Paul's logic:

- To enter salvation, humans must respond to the gospel by acknowledging by faith (trusting loyalty) that Jesus is the Christ (King).
- In the process of becoming the Christ within history, Jesus exerted moral influence over us that inescapably determines what it means to pledge our faith toward him as *that* Christ.
- Part of the specific moral influence over us that Jesus exerted in

becoming the Christ was to show that his own obedient cross-shaped faith (his own trusting loyalty) toward God resulted in his justification and culminated in his resurrection life.

- In light of what happened to Jesus (he was justified by his faith and found life) when he behaved in this way, any who seek justification today have been morally influenced by his example, because they have evidence that Jesus's "by faith" pattern is pleasing to God and results in justification and resurrection life.
- Now any human can imitate Jesus's behavioral pattern by pledging faith (loyalty) to God by pledging faith to his Christ—and in doing so can enter the justified community and enjoy resurrection life.

In short, Jesus's moral influence over us comes before our justification by faith and is basic to it. We are not justified by faith in just any Christ, but by pledging loyalty to the specific Christ who lived and died in a "by faith" way himself. When a person is justified by faith today, they are following Jesus's moral example, for he was justified by faith first. Alongside substitution and *Christus Victor*, moral influence is essential for a complete understanding of the atonement.

(4) Recapitulation

There is another theory of atonement. It seeks to bring all of the others together, but it is also more than the sum of its parts: the recapitulation model.

When you watch the recap of a baseball game or a movie, you are getting the key events, plot twists, and the final outcome in short form. The recapitulation model of the atonement is similar.

Jesus in his kingship is the highlight reel—the recapitulation—as he brings together all that is significant in the story of humans in their relationship with God. As Paul puts it, "all things are *recapitulated* in the Messiah" (Eph. 1:10). The Greek word is *anakephalaioō*—to count the main things up and to reexpress them summarily.

The recapitulation model affirms that King Jesus is the head of a reconstituted humanity. He is a second and final Adam (1 Cor. 15:45). Moreover, in his resurrected and ascended body, Jesus is the first-born from the dead. This implies that he will have many brothers and sisters who likewise will reign with him over the new creation in their resurrected bodies (Col. 1:18; Rom. 8:29). To affirm the recapitulation model of the atonement is to claim that King Jesus saves us by being the head of a reconstituted creation, summing up everything that God intended humanity to be within the old creation.

In speaking of atonement, not only does recapitulation capture key biblical truths regarding how King Jesus summarily reexpresses the plotline of how God relates to humanity, but it is also a helpful metaphor. If we are to appreciate the *why* behind Jesus's death fully yet succinctly, we need to recapitulate—to unite the different models of atonement into one composite image that summarily reexpresses God's reconciling intentions.

In Scripture, the substitutionary, victorious king, and moral influence models of atonement are not in competition but together serve to recap how God is rescuing us. The victorious-king model is presupposed everywhere we see the title "the Christ" applied to the resurrected Jesus. But of course all early Christians knew that this victory came about for us primarily through substitution—the King dying on the cross for our sins.

Yet the moral influence theory of atonement is fundamental for personal salvation too. The justification of an individual by faith today depends on imitating Jesus's pattern of life, for he was justified by his faith first. That is how he became the living Christ-King who can justify us.

The recapitulation model reminds us that God has established King Jesus as the head of a new humanity within his new creation. Recapitulation also encourages us to hold the models of atonement together, viewing what each uniquely contributes to the overall portrait, so we can praise God maximally for his amazing rescue.

3. Raised to Reign

Let's say you are presenting the gospel to a coworker and she is receptive. After telling her about your own past failures and present attempts to follow God, as part of the good news you enthusiastically say, "I believe Jesus the King died for our sins and then rose again!" Well done. These are key portions of the gospel that should be joyfully shared.

Your coworker is aware of her need for God and for life change. So when you share, she is partly on board but has doubts and questions. She says, "I understand that I sin and need God's forgiveness. I admire Jesus's teachings and life. The cross makes sense to me. I'm ready to trust in Jesus's death and to try being his disciple. It's scary—but his ways might be better than what I've been trying."

Yet your coworker continues: "But I don't believe God really raised Jesus from the dead. I believe in science. Until we have evidence that a person who is dead for three days can be brought back to life, I can't make myself believe. I want it to be true, but I can't force myself to believe something so far-fetched."

She looks disheartened. But then she suddenly adds, "But is believing in the resurrection that important? Can't I be saved if I trust Jesus's death for my sins and try to follow him even if I don't believe in the resurrection?"

How would you answer? Is the resurrection really essential to the gospel? Can't a person get into a right relationship with God solely by trusting in Jesus's atoning work on the cross and by embracing his way of life?

These are difficult questions. If you were really having this discussion with a coworker, it could go in several productive directions from here—including one that aims for a more nuanced view of miracles, science, and Christianity. But at least Scripture gives a clear answer to the question about whether the resurrection is really essential to the gospel: emphatically yes. Absolutely.

Resurrection Matters

Scripture presents the historical reality of the Christ's resurrection as essential to the good news and to God's saving work: "If the Christ has not been raised, your faith is useless; you are still in your sins" (1 Cor. 15:17, AT). Paul says the reality of the King's resurrection as a genuine historical event is required for the removal of our sins.

The resurrection is definitely part of the gospel. But is it possible that a person who doesn't believe in the reality of the resurrection, but does trust in the efficacy of Jesus's death for sins, could still be saved through the historical reality of Jesus's resurrection regardless of their disbelief in it?

God only knows. It is difficult to affirm that anyone can be saved who doesn't believe in the resurrection. For example, see Romans 10:9–10. Yet I do know this: When our gospel is all about Jesus on the cross rather than about how Jesus became the Christ, we are not in a good position to help others see why the resurrection matters.

For example, if we think the gospel is all about the cross, it is easy to make the resurrection a miraculous tack-on—a neat proof. But when we think more carefully, we see that such an understanding is flawed. If God's primary purpose in raising Jesus was miraculous certification of Jesus's divinity, the cross's power, or death's defeat, then why would God exalt him subsequently into heaven? Wouldn't we instead expect God to leave Jesus alive and well on earth, so he could serve as perpetual living proof? Moreover, it is not simply Jesus's soul or spirit that goes up. Jesus ascends *in his resurrected body* (Acts 1:9-11).

After Jesus is raised from the dead never to die again, he doesn't simply hang out, like a hand-waving celebrity, to be gawked at by crowds for endless ages. Yes, there are witnesses who see him over a forty-day period and certify the reality of his resurrection—and this is vitally important—but it's not the main point.

When we come to appreciate that the gospel is about how Jesus became King of heaven and earth rather than simply about the cross, Jesus's resurrection makes sense as the essential next step in God's plan to restore his glory over creation. Jesus's resurrection was necessary because creation requires genuine *human* rule.

Resurrected to Reign

The primary purpose of Jesus's resurrection is not to announce God's miraculous power over death or to certify Jesus's divinity— even if those are valid minor purposes. The main purpose of Jesus's resurrection is to permit him to do precisely what he is doing now: ruling as the superlative *human* King at the Father's right hand.

Peter explains the purpose of Jesus's resurrection. It is exaltation for the purpose of ruling: "God has raised this Jesus to life, and we are all witnesses of it. Exalted to the right hand of God, he has received from the Father the promised Holy Spirit and has poured out what you now see and hear" (Acts 2:32–33, NIV).

Jesus is raised so that he can ascend bodily and take up his office as the human ruler over creation.

Although Jesus could appropriately be called the Christ in an anticipatory sense when he was born (Luke 2:11; see also 2:26), God did not "give to him the throne" from which he now rules until after his ascension (see Luke 1:32–33). This is why it is only *after* Jesus's enthronement at the right hand that Peter can conclude: "Therefore let all Israel be assured of this: God has *made* this Jesus, whom you crucified, both *Lord and Messiah*" (Acts 2:36, NIV). When the resurrected Jesus was exalted, he was made the Christ-King in the ultimate sense.

Why the King Needs a Body

It was only upon installation at the Father's right hand *in his resurrected human body* that Jesus began to function authoritatively as the Christ in the full. Remember! God designed creation in such a way that it requires not just divine rule, but *embodied human rule* in order to receive God's complete glory. Creation isn't receiving that ideal human glory until the resurrected Jesus is officially installed as the Christ. In his royal embodied capacity as a human, he can refresh creation. This refreshment happens when humans are changed by gazing on King Jesus, the ideal human.

Actually, Jesus's resurrection and his restored rule over creation are such earth-shattering and reconstituting events that Scripture speaks of the resulting effects as "new creation" (2 Cor. 5:17; Gal. 6:15). The inadequate old elements of creation are created afresh (Col. 2:20; see also Col. 2:8 and Gal. 4:3, 9). Jesus remains fully human (and fully divine) as the resurrected King so he can orchestrate and refresh glory distribution to creation.

Where is Jesus now? *Jesus is in the most authoritative position in the universe, at the Father's right hand in his resurrected body, serving as our King and High Priest.* In those official capacities he is orchestrating the restoration of human glory, so that it comes to reach creation maximally. This is why Paul calls the good news "the gospel of the glory of the Christ" (2 Cor. 4:4). The King's glory is how God receives glory from creation too, as honor is increasingly ascribed to him for creation. So this is also the process by which God is maximally glorified.

From that position King Jesus, along with the Father, sends the Spirit to indwell God's people. The presence of the Spirit is how Jesus's kingship is functionally operative in the midst of God's people. Whenever and wherever Jesus is confessed authentically as Lord or King, there Jesus rules. And he will continue ruling until all his enemies—although they are already vanquished and disarmed—submit to his ultimate authority. His human and divine rule over creation will know no end, for his throne is everlasting. *Jesus was raised to reign.*

We must get the idea out of our heads that the gospel is purposed in the first instance toward *personal* salvation or *individual* rescue. God loves humans—and yes, God's unfathomable love is the deepest reason for the gospel—but he also loves the rest of creation. Individuals are indeed rescued in God's love by the gospel. But they are rescued in part because God needs humans to achieve his creation-wide rescue.

An analogy might help bring together this chapter's leading themes. Think about salvation as a *heart surgery* designed to restore a sick patient.

God loves the sick patient dearly, and that motivates him to act—even to go to the cross in order to provide rescue. But here is the trick: do not think about the patient as an individual person whom God is trying to rescue through the gospel. *The sick patient is creation in its entirety.*

In this analogy humans are still vital. God has a special love for humans as his finest achievement—*humans are the heart of his creation project*—but his love is for all creation. The purpose of the surgery is to save creation as a whole. The required procedure is so radical that what emerges afterward is best termed *new creation*.

Originally a healthy but immature humanity was established by God in creation's heart to distribute glory everywhere. Adam was modeled on the future King that the Father, Son, and Spirit intended to send to be creation's heart once it reached sufficient maturity. Then through this King's leadership, creation would reach its optimal state of glory.

Yet humanity's choice to disobey became a deadly infection, resulting in a premature glory-failure for creation. The death-dealing failure of Adamic humanity was so abject that the patient, creation, had entered a state of morbid decay. So at the time of the King's arrival, God could not bring creation to maturity without deep intervention. A radical surgery became necessary—indeed, a heart transplant, a new humanity. God promised this transplant ahead of time, preparing the operating room by working especially through Abraham's family and David's royal line.

The gospel, then, is the start of the long-awaited heart surgery that saves creation. The gospel is the heart transplant that establishes a new humanity in creation's center. It begins with the incarnation. To fulfill God's intentions for creation, Jesus is sent as the ideal King to show what it means to be truly human—to bear God's glory in all its splendor.

Yet the incarnation on its own does not achieve the necessary transplant. The King, through his obedient life, must be a heart replacement by being all that God intended prior humanity to be (recapitulation). He must win the victory via the cross (*Christus Victor*) by showing a better "by loyalty" way (moral influence) and by carrying the burden of sickness that caused the heart failure for sinful humanity (substitution).

After the King does these things, God justifies Jesus, raising him from the dead—the firstborn of many others—and he is installed bodily at the Father's right hand. Now Jesus serves there as the living human King and High Priest.

Jesus's resurrection and ongoing *human* rule are the heart transplant—the fountainhead of the new creation. Now King Jesus is properly ruling creation on God's behalf, recovering God's intentions for humanity by spreading new creation's glory into the midst of old creation's decay. In other words, the Spirit has been sent. Although the victory has already been won, the King's triumph advances as more and more humans are transformed by allegiance.

QUESTIONS FOR DISCUSSION OR REFLECTION

1. Why is it important to consider that the events that together make up the gospel happened at a specific time in past history before thinking about how the gospel saves individuals today?
2. Why is it essential to recognize that the gospel begins with the incarnation and not with the cross?
3. How does incarnation relate to kingship within the overarching story of Scripture? What was the effect of the fall on incarnation and kingship?

4. Why is the cross nonnegotiably essential to the gospel?

5. Describe something that imprisoned you in the past that King Jesus has redeemed in your life. What is something that currently is imprisoning you that needs redemption? Are there any lessons from your past that can help with your present?

6. Why is *penal* within "penal substitutionary atonement" especially controversial today? Give reasons why some support and others disavow the term.

7. Why is it wrongheaded to suggest that the Father abandoned the Son when he was dying on the cross?

8. What is the *Christus Victor* model of the atonement? Why is it a wider category than substitution?

9. Describe an area of life in which you are struggling to win a victory. How does the *Christus Victor* model speak to you personally?

10. Can you explain the moral influence theory of atonement in your own words? Why is the Christ's moral influence foundational to an individual's justification by faith?

11. Why, beyond the cross, is the bodily resurrection of Jesus essential to the gospel? How does it relate to Jesus's current status? How might this change what it means for you to respond fully to the gospel today?

12. The author describes how the models of atonement interrelate by using the analogy of a heart surgery. Name and briefly describe the four models. Can you think of your own analogy to interrelate them?

Royal Transformation

"I like the gangsters best. . . . O boy, what wouldn't I give to be doing that myself! It's the *life* I tell you." When Mike Teavee chanced upon a ticket, reporters sought interviews. But seated before a ginormous screen watching gangster shows, Mike refused to be interrupted. With eighteen toy guns strapped to his body, he would fire off rounds as the TV programming played on an incessant loop.[1]

Later Willy Wonka showed Mike that he could zap a giant chocolate bar, scatter it over the airwaves, and reconstitute a small edible version of it inside a special TV. Then Mike couldn't be stopped: "Look at me . . . I am going to be the first person in the world to be sent by television!" Heedless of warning, Mike zapped himself and was reconstituted in miniature form within the TV. It did not bother Mike that he had been shrunk to the size of a finger, since this would not prevent him from watching his TV once home. When Mike's horrified parents vowed that his future activities would be different, Mike could only repeatedly squeal, "I want to watch television!"[2]

Mike Teavee's fate may seem grim, but Shel Silverstein tells us the tale of Jimmy Jet, whose endless screen time proved even more transformative. He watched twenty-four hours a day until, first, his eyes were frozen open. Then a metamorphosis proceeded: "his brain turned into TV tubes" and "his face to a TV screen." In the end, his family plugged in Jimmy Jet and proceeded to watch their favorite programs on their brand new but strangely familiar TV set.[3]

Idols may seem ancient, abstract, and irrelevant—that is, until we consider how we spend the majority of our waking hours. After all, a synonym for idol in Scripture is *image*.

If you spend even two minutes on your phone scrolling, you see hundreds of different images—so many that you can only remember a fraction of their ever-shifting variety. Are you doing better than Mike or Jimmy? Tally how many hours you spend viewing images on the screens you own per day—if you dare. This is not a guilt trip; it's a reality check.

Ponder the image-based content that you regularly consume—sometimes with others, but often in private. Think of all the different media: TV shows, movies, video clips, messages, memes, emojis, snapshots. Consider platforms: Facebook, Instagram, Twitter, Snapchat, texts, YouTube, TikTok, Amazon, Netflix, and more.

You've probably made countless viewing choices that you regret. It is impossible to "unsee" powerful images of sex, greed, and violence once they've appeared before our eyes. We can't willfully scrub our memories, even when we desire a fresh start. Once seen, we continue to be affected by powerful images, often in involuntary ways beyond our conscious control.

How is the endless stream of images on your screens training you to *think* about the world—or perhaps even more important, to *feel* about it? We are being transformed by the images that we view.

Even when our viewing choices reflect virtuous content, that content is framed by and interspersed with advertisements. Advertisers are experts at using these images to play with our fantasies, inviting us to picture how our lives will be transformed if we opt to inhabit the scene. What moralities do these images seek to normalize? For social media and other interactive images, what behaviors do they reward?

Images disciple us.

Images disciple us by evoking desire. *Desire* is not worship, but it is a close relative, and a fair index of spiritual health. "You are what you love," as philosopher-theologian James K. A. Smith puts it.[4] We are being transformed into the images that we desirously view and the habits they reinforce.

If we don't first *come* to Jesus—give our primary mental and emotional attention to his glorious image—then we will never *see* in the experiential way necessary to bring about the transformation God desires for us. We must allow our vision of what is good, true, and beautiful to be changed by learning Jesus-shaped habits, and then we must embody these changes through discipleship.

This is how the gospel fits into the true story of the world: Within our real space-and-time history, God sent us a saving King who took on our humanity. He won the victory on the cross and was raised to rule bodily so that he could lead the charge of human transformation in order to refresh creation's glory. So, Jesus's transformative kingship is changing the world from top down.

And yet . . . sigh.

Where is this victorious transformation? When we look around, we see war, toxic relationships, children shot, sexual exploitation, health-care failures, drug problems, abuse, racism, and poverty. If the events that constitute the good news happened more than two thousand years ago, why is the present so ugly?

And yet again . . . wow!

It is not entirely ugly. Pockmarks of Christ-shaped beauty are on display amid the brokenness: when an engineer volunteers to stay late so his coworker can take care of his sick wife; when a nurse rescues her patient's dog from the shelter; when a schoolkid befriends a bullied outcast; when a janitor cleans well even though the boss isn't watching; when a musician sacrifices time to strengthen a praise team; when a relief worker brings medical aid to a war zone. And these are just a few things I've observed Christians doing this month. Who can imagine the unseen piles of goodness? No amount of wickedness can vanquish the radiant deeds of Jesus's people.

King Jesus is at work transforming the world. It's exciting. But we will never understand the *why* of the gospel until we come to appreciate *how Jesus's kingship meaningfully changes individuals as part of glory's slow recovery in the world.*

Stage 5: Transformative Viewing

We've been tracing the glory cycle (for an overview, see chapter 3, p. 57). In the last chapter we arrived at its climax, the gospel. God has already accomplished *in history* a series of events to restore his glory. The gospel is not a timeless truth. The gospel is not that God always wants us to trust him and to stop trying to earn our own salvation. God does want those things, but they aren't the gospel. The gospel is the unmerited grace that God has already given to humanity in the actual world some two thousand years ago *to restore his glory through Jesus's kingship*—and the transformative work he is still doing through the Spirit.

The next portion of the glory cycle—stage five—is *transformative viewing for glory's recovery.* This chapter shows how personal change happens and how it fits within God's wider purposes for world history. We can break this stage of the glory cycle down further. Conveniently stage five has five steps. These five steps describe how *personal change* happens through *seeing.*

The Five Steps of Transformative Viewing

1. The flawless image appears
2. Viewing the ideal image
3. Empowered for transformation

4. Transforming together into the image
5. Conformed to the image

Transformative viewing pertains to the individual but is simultaneously a gradual worldwide process. On the one hand, we need to understand how God's transformative work is slowly unfolding within history. On the other, we need practical guidance, so each of us can fully enter the process today.

1. The Flawless Image Appears

When Jesus took on human flesh on his path toward kingship, he revealed God's glory flawlessly. "The Word became flesh . . . and we have seen his *glory*" (John 1:14, NIV). We have already established that the gospel begins when the Father sends the Son to take on human flesh. The incarnation is the beginning of both the historical and the personal process of recovery. True change becomes possible for individuals and the world when *the glory* of God becomes visible in the perfect human, Jesus.

Flawless How?

But first, we need to know more about how Jesus makes God's glory fully available. "The Son is the image of the invisible God," says the apostle Paul, "For God was pleased to have all his fullness dwell in Him" (Col. 1:15, 19, NIV). Since an image in Paul's culture was a statue or other visual representation, Paul's metaphor suggests that Jesus visually looks *exactly* like the Father. Obviously the point is not that Jesus had black hair, dark eyes, and was five feet, eight inches tall and so the same must be true for the Father. We don't even know what Jesus looked like physically.

Rather Jesus's character qualities mirrored the Father's perfectly—his mercy, justice, and goodness. "Anyone who has seen me,"

Jesus declares, "has seen the Father" (John 14:9). When a person truly sees Jesus—his virtues on the inside, not his physical characteristics on the outside—they see all the Father's qualities in a precise, concrete fashion.

Although there were prior clues, it was the events that together constitute the gospel that first revealed the Trinity to humanity.[5] As part of the gospel, the Father sent his Son, and then they sent the Spirit. They are three persons, but there is only one God. The three are one God because they are the same substance or essence. That is, whatever it means to be God, they all three are that fully. Meanwhile Jesus is human and divine, completely both, because he has each nature. All the Father's fullness dwells in Jesus, because the Son's eternal unchanging divine person assumed Jesus's complete human nature in the incarnation.

Dynamic Representation

We tend to think of images as stationary, but Scripture depicts the process of imaging as dynamic, because it reveals glory. As the author of Hebrews puts it, "The Son is the radiance of God's glory and the exact representation of his being" (1:3, NIV). In Greek the word *apaugasma*—here translated "radiance"—also means *effulgence* or *reflection*. In this word picture the Father is the source of overwhelmingly brilliant glory and the Son is the agent through whom that splendor reaches us—whether as a beam or a reflected image.

This portrayal of the Son as actively glorious is supplemented by calling him, "the exact representation of God's being" (1:3, NIV). In Greek the phrase is *charaktēr tēs hypostaseōs*. The word *charaktēr* pertains to minting coins. An exact visual imitation was required between the stamp and the soft metal in order to press an image into a coin. The Son is this *charaktēr*, this exact visual representation, that emerges from God the Father.

Here, then, Jesus is said to represent God the Father exactly. But with respect to what? His *hypostasis*. That is, the Father's foundational substance or constitutive being. Hebrews indicates that whatever the Father's basic reality might be—whatever the divine "is-ness" of Father is—the Son emerges from that imprint.

The Son is fully God from all eternity. In formulating a full doctrine of the Trinity, we must harmonize this passage with others that show that the Father did not radiate or mint the Son at a specific point in time. The Nicene Creed was written in the fourth century in an attempt to close off the Arian heresy—which claimed that the Son was a creature begotten at a specific point in time by the Father.

Arianism was judged a heresy—correctly—because Scripture attests that the Father *eternally* produces the Son in a fatherly fashion and that the Son has *his own eternal glory* alongside him (for example, Ps. 2:5–9; John 1:1–3, 1:14; 16:28; 17:5; Heb. 1:5; 5:5). This is why the Nicene Creed asserts that although the Father begets the Son eternally, they are of the same essence or substance (*homoousios*). The Father, Son, and Spirit always have been, and always will be, the one true God.

Taken together these passages remind us that when we gaze on the Son, since he is fully God, the image is perfect. So when we behold him we are able to see the undistorted fullness of the Father.

2. Viewing the Ideal Image

Now let's get practical. How do we get into a position to see Jesus's internal qualities, so that this transformative viewing might take place? We must *come into his presence* with an intention to be disciples.

Present for Viewing

In the early phases of Jesus's ministry, two men started following him. Jesus noticed, spun around, and abruptly confronted them: "What do you want?" They indicated their desire to be mentored by saying, "Rabbi, where are you staying?" (John 1:37–38). These men correctly recognized that in order to adopt Jesus's ways, it was needful not simply to hotfoot behind him along the road but *to stay in his presence*. They needed to see and experience his whole manner of life.

Jesus's reply to these men is a fitting invitation for all would-be disciples: "*Come* and you will *see*" (John 1:39). If we want to be disciples of Jesus we need to cultivate practices that will help us *enter into his presence* so that we can *see*. Personal transformation begins when we *draw near* to Jesus with the intention of discipleship, so we can *observe* how Jesus lived.

Intentional Seeing

Intentional seeing is necessary for three reasons. First, without intentionality we will only discover the Jesus who we already prefer. We urgently want to discover that we—and the people we admire— have been right all along in our values, morality, social choices, and politics. Confirmation bias and self-centered rationalization seem to know no limits. Without intentionality, we will only find the Jesus we want—the one who doesn't ask us to change—rather than the Jesus who longs to transform us.

Second, apart from intentionality the true Jesus will remain hidden, buried by secular agendas. The world—and sadly large sectors of the church too—have managed to wrap Jesus, mummy-like, in a thousand layers of disguise. Everyone wants to mobilize Jesus for their agenda—you can find patriotic Jesus, suburban Jesus, LGBTQ Jesus, feminist Jesus, woke Jesus, gun-rights Jesus, tolerant Jesus, and many other caricatures. We must be deliberate if we are to peel away the costumery. With so many competing agendas, the authentic Jesus can seem elusive.

Third, unless we are singularly purposed in viewing Jesus, we will not see enough of him to have our affections changed. If we don't *want* to be a disciple of Jesus, then we won't be. It is that simple. We won't change if we don't want to change—if we can't see enough of the higher good toward which Jesus is pointing that we come to *desire* it. Intentionality in viewing Jesus is imperative, because without it we will never discover what *he loves*, and why—and in so doing have our own desires forged anew.

Given the urgency of intentionality and these obstacles, how can we foster it? There is no substitute for the Bible. We must turn to Scripture's depictions of Jesus—again and again, always returning

> *If we don't want to be a disciple
> of Jesus, then we won't be.
> It is that simple.*

to it—to refine our image of Jesus, or else we will be viewing a distortion. Fortunately, Jesus and his apostles carefully deposited the foundational building blocks for discipleship so that subsequent generations could indeed *come* and *see*.

Beyond Scripture there are also guides to assist us. I've mentioned a number of helpful voices already in this book, including C. S. Lewis, N. T. Wright, Scot McKnight, and Carmen Imes. Ancient apprentices to Jesus—writers like Irenaeus, Augustine, and Thomas à Kempis—remain helpful. The works of Dallas Willard and Richard Foster are already modern classics. Contemporary authors like Tim Keller, Tish Harrison Warren, Esau McCauley, John Mark Comer, and Richard Villodas are thoughtfully equipping many. Creative Christians are using emerging media to reach an ever-expanding audience: Andrew Peterson (through his music and books), Tim Mackie and Jon Collins (*The Bible Project* videos and podcast), Phil Vischer and Skye Jethani (*The Holy Post* podcast), John Dickson (*Undeceptions* podcast), and Justin Brierley (*Unbelievable* on Premier Christian Radio).

In sum, a deliberate and accurate viewing of Jesus is an essential first step toward discipleship. Beginning with Scripture, we must look intently at how the ideal human lived—his teachings, practices, and life trajectory—if we are to have any hope that we might find ourselves reminted into his image. What do we see once we are positioned in Jesus's presence?

Disciple-Making for Relational Wisdom

When we gaze on Jesus with a readiness to be changed, above all else we discover not rules but *relational wisdom*. Once trained by Jesus's relational wisdom, we can step into what Jonathan Pennington, in his book on Jesus's Sermon on the Mount, calls "true human flourishing."[6] In the midst of a broken world, this flourishing can become available for ourselves and others.

We have so much to learn from Jesus: how to pray, teach, lead, serve, forgive, confront injustice, and treat enemies. The list could go on *ad infinitum*. Jesus's alternative values teach us how to be subversively wise.

Yet since the goal is to come and see in order to become his followers, we should take special note of what Jesus explicitly taught about discipleship. What it means to be a disciple is the focus in the following subsections.

A Cross-Shaped Path

Jesus indicates that if anyone wants to be his disciple, that person must "deny himself, take up his cross, and follow me" (Matt. 16:24; see also Mark 8:34 and Luke 14:27). This means radically renouncing the self's rights, prerogatives, and comforts in order to serve others—to the point of death. Luke reminds us that cross-bearing is not a once-in-a-lifetime decision, but a "daily" task (9:23).

For Jesus's first disciples, this often included acceptance of temporary homelessness (Matt. 8:19–20), following Jesus even when it meant that basic obligations of law or decency could not be met (Matt. 8:21–22), valuing Jesus above family (Matt. 10:34–39), and trusting God to meet daily needs in the midst of mission (Matt. 10:9–10).

To be a disciple of Jesus means to serve all (Mark 9:35). It includes taking the lowest seat—to be least and last—humbling oneself while trusting that God exalts his servants at the proper time (Luke 14:7–11). It means undertaking menial tasks like foot washing, tasks reserved for lowly slaves (John 13:1–17).

The basic requirement for being a disciple is, as a deliberate act of loyalty and self-denial, to walk in the footsteps of your King toward the cross, trusting that it will prove to be the path to true life for yourself and others.

Not Generic but for Jesus

Yet don't be fooled. Self-denial as its own end leads to a dead end. Self-denial should never be simply for self-denial's sake. Paul says that self-denial that is not rooted in King Jesus has an appearance of wisdom, but ultimately it fails because not only is it wrongly aimed, but it is also underpowered (Col. 2:20–23). Since it is not Spirit-led, it doesn't stop our fleshly appetites. When self-denial is not targeted correctly, it does not result in transformation.

Let me put it another way: the path of the cross is not *general* self-denial but must be specifically for Jesus. To take up the cross is not that *we should all remember to give back*, or *we ought to help others*, or *we all have to put up with obnoxious people while acting charitably*. Rather to take up the cross means we should all remember to give back *because Jesus did*, or we ought to help others *because Jesus was a servant*, or we all have to put up with obnoxious people—*and I am chief among them—so I need to change to become like Jesus*.

As Jesus himself puts it, discipleship is life-giving only when a person seeks to die to the self deliberately "for *my* sake" and for "*the gospel's* sake" (Mark 9:35). That is, in Jesus's own words, taking up the cross is not life-giving when it devolves into a general principle of self-sacrifice, but only when it is intentionally an act of following him.

Beyond making self-denial its own end, it is easy to misfire in another way. We can become falsely convinced that self-denial is only for the good of others rather than for our own good too. If we don't understand the *liberating* purposes behind Jesus's demand to deny ourselves, we wrongly become convinced that God perversely delights in snatching away any sliver of happiness we might enjoy. Then God becomes a cosmic Grinch who chortles with glee when I suffer for someone else yet bear it with an undefeated half-smile.

Self-denial doesn't work unless it is an act of loyalty to Jesus and his gospel, because true freedom can only be found under his banner. We die to ourselves in the King, because the new self that emerges is increasingly liberated from sin (Rom. 6). Paul summarizes, "I have been crucified with the King. It is no longer I who live, but the King who lives in me. The life I now live in the flesh I live by loyalty unto the Son of God, who loved me and gave himself for me" (Gal. 2:20, AT). We find genuine freedom when, by faith, we confess Jesus as King, while walking in step with the Spirit (Rom. 8:1–17). Because it unites us to his death and resurrection power, the way of the cross proves to be the path of liberation as we come under Jesus's sovereign sway.

A Daily and Lifelong Cost

To take up the cross is both a lifelong trajectory and a daily task. Death is not easy or glib. So Jesus warns us that we must count the cost from the outset to make sure we are determined to complete the process; otherwise it will be to no avail.

Jesus compares discipleship to constructing a tower: anyone who doesn't make sure up front that they are willing to pay for the project will be proven a fool when the half-built tower is abandoned (Luke 14:27–30). He further compares it to a king contemplating a war. Unless the king calculates that he can afford what victory will cost, it would be stupid to start the battle (Luke 14:31–32). So also, Jesus says, "any one of you who does not renounce all that he has is not able to be my disciple" (Luke 14:33, AT). Half-measures will fail. Discipleship will cost your all.

Ironically though, counting the cost strengthens our resolve. Jesus reminds us that although dying to your present self is pricey, careful accounting shows it to be a savvy deal. We'll have to give up our present selves at the end of life. Only cross-carrying disciples of Jesus will be fit for life in the new age that God is ushering in (Mark 8:35–37). It makes little sense to cling to any non-Jesus portions of ourselves.

When we calculate sagely, we die so that we can live. When we die to our present self by taking up the cross, we get more back because we are transformed—and the new self we gain *right now* is permeated by an eternal quality of life that is suited for the resurrection age (John 5:24). Those who take up the cross daily for Jesus's sake will find King Jesus issuing a verdict in their favor at the final judgment (Mark 8:38).

Why is a positive response to the gospel still the best choice a person can ever make? Death to the self for King Jesus's sake proves to be the only investment that yields true life now and forevermore.

To Obey Him as King

Obedience is the hallmark of genuine discipleship. Jesus says "anyone who loves me will obey my teaching" (John 14:23). Not only does obedience accurately measure our love for Jesus, but it also indicates the presence of true life for a disciple (John 8:51). The apostle John puts it starkly: "Whoever has faith [*pisteuōn*] in the Son has eternal life; whoever does not *obey* the Son shall not see life, but the wrath of God remains on him" (John 3:36, AT). In other words, when we express believing loyalty—"faith" (*pistis*)—we enter into the eternal quality of life that belongs to the Son. And this believing loyalty correlates with obedience to him.

Obeying Jesus's Person

We are summoned to obey Jesus on the basis of his person and his attainment of universal authority. Even before being officially enthroned as the Christ at the Father's right hand, Jesus commanded obedience by virtue of his person. Storms, wind, water, and waves submitted to Jesus (see Luke 8:25). Surely his disciples would be wise to do likewise? Evil spirits that opposed Jesus nevertheless fearfully obeyed him (Mark 1:27). How much more should those obey who are seeking to advance Jesus's agenda?

Obeying Jesus's Office

Yet after Jesus's death and resurrection, obedience to Jesus is demanded not only by his person, but also by his official status. After being raised, Jesus summoned his followers in order to tell them that he now has *all authority*—both in heaven and on earth. In other words, Jesus announced his installation as the King of kings. Then he told his disciples to make other disciples by "*teaching them to obey everything that I have commanded you*" (Matt. 28:20, NIV).

This passage teaches us three things about obedience: First, to be a disciple of Jesus today is to recognize that he appropriately holds all authority. To choose freely to obey is not merely our duty, but also our privilege and delight, since he is the one fully good and highest King forever. *Jesus's authority as King to command obedience is unrivaled.*

Second, the extent to which Jesus rightfully commands obedience knows no bounds. Jesus has authority *everywhere*—heaven and earth—and we are to obey *everything* that he commands. *The scope of Jesus's demand for obedience is limitless.*

Third, Jesus anticipates that obedience will not come automatically. His words, "*teach them* to obey," indicate an imperfect process. Jesus knew that our obedience would not be flawless or instantaneous. Obedience is part of the learning dimension of discipleship. Jesus wore a crown of thorns for a reason. He wanted to show that he is a forgiving King who is endlessly *for us* in the midst of our sinful mistakes as we learn how to obey. *Because it must be learned, Jesus's disciples will be imperfect in their obedience.*

King Jesus as the Law's Embodiment

Granted that disciples are learning to be obedient, how does discipleship relate to the specific commandments that God had already given his people prior to Jesus's incarnation? We know from Scripture that certain portions of the Mosaic law have been climactically fulfilled—like kosher laws—so that they are no longer universally binding on God's people (Mark 7:19; Acts 10:9–16; Rom. 14:20). We also know that we can't earn salvation by performing the law. As the apostle Paul puts it, "Since by works of the law no flesh will be justified in God's sight" (Rom. 3:20, AT; see also Gal. 2:16).

While we do not enter into a right relationship with God by performing the letter of the law—whether the law of Moses or the new law given by King Jesus—nevertheless obedience to the King's royal law proves to be life-giving. Jesus said, "Do not think that I have come to abolish the Law or the Prophets; I have not come to abolish them but to fulfill them" (Matt. 5:17, NIV). His kingship does not dissolve God's prior laws, but rather fulfills them.

Jesus's fulfillment of the law is possible because "the virtuous king submits himself to the laws and thereby internalizes them such that he himself becomes an embodiment of the law—a 'living law'"—as theologian Joshua Jipp describes it.[7] It is also why Jesus speaks of the law positively. As the climactic King, Jesus is the embodiment and culmination of all that God intended in giving his prior law.

The Christ is the living law. To be a disciple, then, means to fulfill the law's deepest intentions too in imitation of Jesus. This is why a follower of Jesus, like Paul, can state that he is not "apart from the law of God but *in the law* of the Christ" (1 Cor. 9:20, AT). Moreover, Paul sees submission to the law of the Christ as fulfilling God's legal intentions (Gal. 6:2). James says much the same in speaking of "the law that gives freedom" (1:25; 2:12) while affirming the Christian urgency to keep the "the royal law" as found in Scripture and echoed by Jesus (2:8). Disciples keep Jesus's royal law not to earn salvation, but because they are allegiant. Disciples are able to do this not through legalistic rule-keeping, but through following the Spirit's lead.

How does Jesus teach his followers to become God's living law? In a series of sayings in his Sermon on the Mount, Jesus takes up some famous Old Testament teachings—for example, "do not murder," "do not commit adultery," and "eye for eye." But in each case, Jesus radicalizes it to show God's true intentions. Jesus tells his followers that they are indeed to obey the actual command. Yet they must push beyond superficial obedience in order to live out the foundational reason why God gave that law.

In imitation of their King, Jesus's disciples must come to embody God's deepest intentions for his law. Jesus makes this clear in the three examples that follow.

Love rather than Murder

Jesus's disciples are to become the living law first by reflecting on God's purpose in giving a specific law. Jesus points out that God gave a command: "You shall not murder" (Matt. 5:21; see Exod. 20:13). God did this because he doesn't want humans to kill one another wrongfully.

Yet this wasn't God's only or even his deepest reason in issuing this command: God would have us love others in such a way that we never become angry enough with a brother or sister so that we would desire to commit a murder. God doesn't merely want a lack of murder. God wants a lack of the kind of anger and vengeful desire that results in murder. God wants a heartfelt obedience from his people, a desire to keep his law that has been written on the heart.

Sexual Purity rather than Adultery

God is not a killjoy. God said, "You shall not commit adultery" (Matt. 5:27; see Exod. 20:14) not because he disapproves of sex, but so that our internal sexual desire will be in harmony with external behavior that leads to flourishing for everyone.

God created us to have sex. But God forbids adultery because he wants us to come to appreciate that sex outside of marriage is selfish and harmful to ourselves and society. It is not in accord with relational wisdom that leads to the blessed life. God wants us to discern his goodness in instituting marriage and in forbidding adultery to such a degree that our lust for extramarital activities is entirely quenched. In interpreting the "no adultery" law, Jesus wants his disciples to conform to that law from the inside out.

Forgiveness rather than Revenge

Similarly, God's "eye for eye" command was designed to maintain justice while limiting revenge in ancient Israel (Matt. 5:38; see Exod. 21:24; Lev. 24:20; Deut. 19:21). But God gave it to shape his people holistically. Jesus tells us that the Father's deeper rationale was that our hearts be captured by his forgiveness ethic. To be a disciple of Jesus means to imitate him in forgiving enemies—indeed not just forgiving, but praying for our enemies.

In our King, our desire to take revenge should be so distant that we would rather be doubly wronged than to seek it. If hit on one cheek, the follower of Jesus should willingly present the other. If forced to go one mile, we should go two (Matt. 5:39–41). We are to act in imitation of our King, who proved he had internalized God's law when he said, "Father, forgive them, for they do not know what they are doing" (Luke 23:34, NIV). Jesus is a living law because as the ideal King he embodies the truest purposes of God's laws.

Because the King lives out the law's deepest intentions, disciples of Jesus press beyond superficial obedience to God's law to a heartfelt obedience. It is a learning process that, for success, depends on the power of the Holy Spirit to write God's law on the human heart within Jesus's new covenant (Jer. 31:31–34; Luke 22:20; 2 Cor. 3:6). It will involve setbacks, failures, and acts of disloyalty. But Spirit-led obedience to Jesus is the hallmark of discipleship and eternal life.

To Love God and Keep the Golden Rule

There is a further implication of Jesus serving as God's living law. When Jesus was asked about the greatest commandment, he did not need to innovate. Although some of God's specific directives may change situationally to reflect the vagaries of human history, God's fundamental moral purposes for humanity are unchanging.

Thus, when asked, Jesus did not create a new rule. Jesus was able to draw from the heart of the Old Testament's teaching, showing that God's purposes for us are consistent. "Jesus replied: 'Love the Lord your God with all your heart and with all your soul and with all your mind.' This is the first and greatest commandment" (Matt. 22:37–38, NIV; see Deut. 6:5). Jesus simply reproclaimed the greatest commandment.

But Jesus wasn't finished. Although he had only been prompted to give the greatest command, he knew that it would be incomplete without its complement: "And the second is like it: 'Love your neighbor as yourself'" (Matt. 22:38–39, NIV; see Lev. 19:18). The first is incomplete apart from the second because God is concerned both with *how we relate to him* and *how we treat one another.*

Sometimes, especially when we've been mistreating others or failing to serve, we try to tell ourselves: all that really matters is that I trust in Jesus so that I'm right with God. At other times, especially when we are trying to justify our slovenly worship habits, we'll try to tell ourselves: all that really matters to God is how I treat other people.

The truth is they are interconnected: the first is the most essential command because right behavior flows from true worship of the living God. If I am responding in love to the one true God, that will spill over, generating love for others. Disciples will love God and neighbor. Jesus says, "All the Law and the Prophets hang on these two commandments" (Matt. 22:40, NIV).

To Be Single-Minded

Jesus's emphasis on fulfilling the law reminds us that discipleship does not stop at proper beliefs; it is active. Jesus expects his disciples to give charitably, pray, and fast. But Jesus makes it clear that his disciples are not to act like the hypocrites. Righteous deeds are for God rather than for human approval (Matt. 6:1–18). Jesus's disciples are to give, pray, and fast not to earn human glory, but in a nonflamboyant fashion to win honor before God.

Disciples are to be single-minded in their devotion to God. They are to store up treasures in heaven rather than on earth, to keep their eyes light-filled by aiming them at God's things, and they must serve God rather than money (Matt. 6:19–24). Anyone who thinks it is possible to serve God and money will discover that double-mindedness is doomed to fail. We will be forced to choose a master. By observing God's faithfulness in caring for his lesser creatures, disciples learn to trust in God's present and future provision rather than to worry (Matt. 6:25–33). The Father is good and knows our needs even before we ask.

A follower of Jesus does not merely hear Jesus's words, nor does a disciple merely say "Lord, Lord." Rather, he or she fruitfully puts Jesus's words into practice (Matt. 7:15–27).

To Bear Witness to His Kingship

To imitate Jesus means to attest to Jesus's kingship. Jesus spent the bulk of his public ministry announcing that the kingdom of God had drawn near: he was testifying that he was in the process of becoming the human who would rule on God's behalf in an ultimate sense. Therefore, when we tell others about Jesus's kingship we are following Jesus.

Disciples follow Jesus when they call people from *different nations, ethnicities, and cultures* to give allegiance to Jesus. Jesus did not invite a select few elites to acknowledge his kingship. The welcome was first extended to his own people—Jews, whom he called "the lost sheep of Israel" (Matt. 15:24)—but Jesus expanded the circle to show that his kingship involved the welcome of non-Jews too (for example, Mark 7:24–31; Luke 10:33; 17:11–19; John 4:7; 10:16).

Jesus invited everyone—poor, rich, male, female—but he made a special effort to let *outcasts* know that they were welcome. Those who were marginal, deemed lesser, or sinful: prostitutes, tax collectors, Samaritans, gentiles, women; those with illnesses, skin diseases, disabilities, and disfigurements. He not only welcomed them, but he also greeted them, touched them, and took on their infirmities (Matt. 8:17). His disciples should do likewise.

Of course, although all are invited, receiving God's gracious invitation is not equivalent to accepting it by pledging faith. A grace—a gift—must be received or else it is in vain (see 1 Cor. 15:2; 2 Cor. 6:1; Heb. 12:15). Disciples testify in hope that Jesus's offer of rescuing kingship and clemency will be accepted by everyone, but they know their King leaves people free to choose in the present. Even so, disciples remember that nobody is free from the *future consequences* of their present choices.

Thus, to be a disciple of Jesus, to follow his pattern of life, means accepting the gift of Jesus's kingship while bearing witness to it. To share the gospel is not separate from discipleship but is part of its substance.

Bearing Witness Then and Now

Generally, disciples today should follow the evangelistic pattern established by Jesus and his first followers. But this must be qualified in one crucial way. We must recognize that what it means for a follower of Jesus to bear witness accurately to Jesus's kingship is not exactly the same for Jesus's first followers as it is for us now. This is true because his status changed between the incarnation and ascension.

To bear witness accurately as disciples today, we must attend to Jesus's new status. When he first took on human flesh, Jesus was and remained God's Son. He was the chosen Christ albeit still awaiting his throne. At first Jesus didn't want those he healed or his disciples to tell others about him (as in Mark 1:43–44; 3:12; Luke 9:21). His kingship was different. Heralding it prematurely would only cause confusion.

Once the suffering nature of kingship was clarified, Jesus could be heralded as the coming servant King who represents the Father (for example, Luke 10:1–24, especially verse 16). After his ascension, he could be attested further: he is the "Son-of-God-in-Power," the installed Christ, the King who is officially ruling heaven and earth (Rom. 1:4; Acts 2:36; Eph. 1:10; Phil. 2:10–11).

Upon his ascension, while remaining the divine Son, Jesus came to possess all ruling authority beyond what he previously held as the divine Son. Now he is the divine *and human* ruler, the Christ. The gospel of his kingship is the premier grace, the fundamental gift that God has given to the world. We accept this gift by pledging loyalty to this King by becoming his disciple. Discipleship includes choosing the path of the cross, aiming to God-please rather than people-please, becoming a living expression of God's law, staying single-minded, obeying Jesus, loving God and neighbor, and attesting to Jesus's kingship.

3. Empowered for Viewing

The disciples came and saw. They intimately experienced Jesus and imitated him in his daily life. Jesus taught them how to be ideal humans: to live the cruciform life, fulfill the law's deepest intention, seek God's approval, bear witness to Jesus's kingship, and to love God and neighbor. But when Jesus was arrested and their own necks were at risk, what happened?

They all fled.

Peter, the leading apostle, denied Jesus three times.

What went wrong?

Before Pentecost, although many had acknowledged Jesus's emerging kingship in an anticipatory way, the full power of the gospel was not yet available. Since Jesus had not been enthroned, the events that constitute the whole gospel had not yet happened in history. At Pentecost, because Jesus has now been enthroned, he is able along with the Father to pour out the Holy Spirit, creating a saved *group*. It is in this group and this group alone that definitive transformation and glory's recovery are ensuing.

In other words, although to come and see is the necessary starting place for transformative discipleship, it alone is not enough. It is not possible to stay allegiant to the King apart from God's special assistance. Peter had confessed Jesus as the Christ. But before Peter could fully follow his King along the cross-marked path, Jesus had to tread it first.

The power of sin, law, and the old order had to be decisively broken within history by Jesus on the cross. Only then could his disciples follow by taking up their crosses too. The King has ushered in this new era. We enter it by giving allegiance.

In order to join the Holy Spirit community, we must transfer allegiance by repenting from other loyalties and pledging faith instead to King Jesus. Once we have turned to the Lord, his Holy Spirit power becomes available, so that fully transformative viewing of the King can transpire: "All of us who with *unveiled* faces are beholding as in a mirror the *glory* of the Lord are being *transformed* into *the same image* from *glory* into *glory*" (2 Cor. 3:18, AT). Notice the necessity of first attaining an *unveiled* face.

The presence of Jesus's flawless image alone is *not* what causes transformation. It is only effective for those with unveiled faces. Paul explains how we come to have unveiled faces, saying: "only through the Christ is the veil taken away" (2 Cor. 3:14) and "whenever a person turns to the Lord the veil is removed" (3:16). That is, the veil is removed when a person repents from self-rule and acknowledges Jesus as Lord, for then the Spirit of the enthroned Lord begins to reign—and we are set free (3:17). When we commit to Jesus's kingship, sin's power is broken (Rom. 6). The definitive starting place for personal transformation is a saving response to the King Jesus gospel.

Yet once we have become unveiled, the process of transformative viewing still isn't automatic. We must participate by *actively viewing Jesus's image*: "And all of us who with unveiled faces are beholding as in a mirror the glory of the Lord are being transformed" (2 Cor. 3:18, AT). In other words, *intentional gazing for the purpose of change* is key. When unveiled viewers *behold* Jesus's glory something begins to happen to us: we can't help but desire more of it, so *our own image is transformed into the glorious image of Jesus.*

4. Transforming Together into the Image

Transformative viewing is a group process. It happens especially when the people of God—the church—view Jesus together. God is very much concerned with rescuing individuals. But God accomplishes this not by saving this or that individual via a personal transaction and then hoping they find each other to create a community. Rather, *God has already constituted the saved community— the church—within history by pouring out the Spirit on individuals as they were gathered as a group.*

Pentecost established a saved group. It is impossible for any single individual today to be saved apart from entering the group that is already being saved, because the Holy Spirit invisibly unites all those who are allegiant to Jesus.

We stare at the image of Jesus best when we do it together—in community—because we are able to reveal different aspects of Jesus's fullness to one another. "If the whole body were an eye, where would be the sense of hearing? If the whole body were an ear, where would be the sense of smell?" (1 Cor. 12:17, AT). In community, we can rebuke false private images of King Jesus while encouraging true holistic image formation.

When we actively gaze on Jesus's glorious image, we are transformed *together* into his image. But this is not an instantaneous transformation. It happens slowly by degrees, "from glory into glory." This is why personal and communal transformation is a lengthy process.

5. Conformed to the Image

There will usually be some sudden and dramatic changes in an individual when they switch allegiance away from the self in favor of Jesus's kingship. Sin's power is now broken. Right now we are new creatures in the King.

Yet suddenly liberated creatures must learn unfamiliar habits. Strange new virtues must be cultivated. We must learn to put on "the new self, which is being renewed in knowledge in *the image* of its Creator" (Col. 3:10, NIV). Our knowledge must be renewed, leading to conformity to the image.

Whether new recruits or old hands, disciples have much to learn from Jesus—and that takes time and mutual glory refreshment within community. We must continue staring at Jesus's image together in order for our own images to be transformed increasingly into his glorious image.

Beholding the Unveiled Splendor

But one day, the King will return. Then we will see him in his unveiled splendor, and our transformation into his image will reach completion.

We don't know all the details of how we will change at that time. The apostle John says that although we presently are God's children, our final transformation remains somewhat mysterious: "Dear friends, now we are children of God, and what we will be has not yet been made known." Yet whatever mystery remains, John says we know the outcome: "But we know that when the Christ appears, we will be like him, for we will see him just as he is" (1 John 3:2, AT).

Did you catch that?

The key to our final transformation is seeing the Christ fully. When he returns, that will happen. We shall see him as he is, and we shall be changed so that we are like him. Paul describes it similarly, "For now we see only a reflection as in a mirror; then we shall see *face to face.* Now I know in part; then *I shall know fully*, even as I am fully known" (1 Cor. 13:9, NIV). Once the King returns, we will see him face to face. That will cause a full knowing that will coincide with a final conformation to his glorious image.

Fully matching the image of the King, who is the image of God, we will be fit to reign alongside Jesus forever. When we receive this good news, we can't help but be drawn into worship.

Worship, Worship, Worship

Our final transformation into the royal image of King Jesus begins and ends with worship. When we see Jesus for who he really is—the King of kings and the Lord of lords, the lion of the tribe of Judah who is worthy because he is simultaneously the slain lamb—then we can't help but be drawn into worship:

> Worthy is the lamb, who was slain,
>> to receive power and wealth and
>> wisdom and strength
>> and honor and glory and praise! (Rev. 5:12, NIV)

The book of Revelation is replete with worship, because its author, the apostle John, knew that worship itself is a form of gazing—attending to the truth about King Jesus. Worship is not without transforming effect.

We attain the final stage of transformation in and through our ongoing praise of the Christ, because when we enter true worship, the veil is snatched away. Our best Christian songwriters have recognized this:

> Soar we now where Christ has led, Alleluia!
> Following our exalted Head, Alleluia!
> Made like him, like him we rise, Alleluia!
> Ours the cross, the grave, the skies, Alleluia![8]

When we worship through such songs, we see the Christ for who he really is: victorious through the cross, triumphant over death, reigning in power. When we adore his kingly splendor, we are "made like him" in such a way that "like him we rise." We rediscover our true position, that we are indeed seated in the Christ at the right hand, exalted to rule in glory alongside King Jesus when he appears in his final glory (Col. 3:1–4).

Worship is a vehicle that allows us to conform to the image of King Jesus, so that we enter into his rule. Christian songwriter Graham Kendrick reminds us that it is only when we gaze on Jesus's "kingly brightness" that we come to display his "likeness." We are transformed as we stare at the radiance of the King. This transformation is from one degree of *glory* into another, as the apostle Paul reminds us (2 Cor. 3:18). Worship helps us gaze upon the King so that our lives come to reflect his glorious life to such a degree that *our story* becomes an announcement of *his story*: "Mirrored here may our lives tell your story."[9] It is *worship itself* that draws us into the divine life, so that our lives reflect the glory that God intends.

Our worship will never cease, for worship holds us in conformity to the image of the King into which we have been transformed. When we worship King Jesus, contemplating his royal majesty, we reflect the King's royal splendor in our own lives, so that others have the chance to enter the King's story too. In the new Jerusalem that will one day descend from heaven, those who belong to God and the lamb will appear before the throne, and "will worship him" (Rev. 22:3, NIV). "They will *see* his face . . . and they will *reign* forever and ever" (Rev. 22:4–5, NIV).

In the end, humans will remain in conformity to the image of the Son as they continually worship. Creation will experience the glory as we rule over it with and under King Jesus. Come, Lord Jesus.

> Hallelujah!
>   For our Lord God Almighty reigns.
> Let us rejoice and be glad
>   and give him glory!
> For the wedding of the Lamb has come,
>   and his bride has made herself ready.
>   (Rev. 19:6–7, NIV)

I'm certainly not in a position to be preachy about the images I've chosen to view. I've made and continue to make choices that I regret. But can I share with you the single *best* viewing choice I have ever made as a disciple of Jesus?

When I was a senior in college I lived by myself for a year. I rented a basement apartment from a middle-aged couple who lived on the edge of the forest outside of Spokane. I loved it!—nature, beauty, solitude, stillness. I hated it!—isolation, boredom, my own obsessive-compulsive thoughts and desires constantly gnawing.

I decided to try an experiment. I threw away my TV. It wasn't that I thought TV was all that bad. But I knew I was hiding behind it, using it to stave off the loneliness. Also, a Christian mentor I admired didn't own one. I tried reading instead. But that didn't work well on its own. When I wasn't reading, the swirl of self-absorbed thoughts would overwhelm me.

So I determined that as a replacement for TV, I would try to memorize Scripture when the loneliness, boredom, and narcissism started to consume. I hoped these actions would prove to be a small step to improve my walk with the Lord.

It was more transformative than I could have imagined. I started out slowly and tentatively with short passages. My appetite grew. Eventually I memorized whole books of the Bible. What occupied my mind more than anything during that year was Jesus's teachings and the apostle Paul's moral injunctions.

I found that what I came to value and want—my yearnings and strivings—began to realign significantly. Rather than wanting a prestigious high-paying job, I wanted a job that would make an impact for Jesus. Rather than wanting to make money so I could ski every weekend, I wanted to use my weekends to help others encounter Jesus through Bible studies. My mind was infused with Scripture. I didn't know it at the time, but I was doing image-replacement therapy.

After that year of detoxing from TV and replacing it with Scripture's images, I have never had a real desire to go back. I own a TV today, but I do not have it permanently set up. If I want to watch something, I have to fetch the TV, move it into place, and plug in various things. I do watch occasionally—OK—more than occasionally, counting baseball. (Baseball is the perfect sport and therefore must be holy. Can I get an "amen"?) But the extra effort to set up the TV reminds me: How will what I view affect me spiritually? I have learned that what I choose to view will ineluctably shape my thoughts and desires.

Somehow I need to make sure that I will view King Jesus *more*.

QUESTIONS FOR DISCUSSION OR REFLECTION

1. What visual images do you see most frequently? How do they make you feel? What behaviors do they encourage?
2. What sources supply the images that appear before your eyes most frequently? Who chooses them and why? How can you take firmer control over the images you choose to view?
3. What do you want most in life? If someone were to observe you for twenty-four hours a day for an entire week, what would they say you want most? How can you change what you desire?
4. What does it mean to call Jesus the flawless image? Why might this be important for your personal transformation?
5. Do you struggle more to *draw near* to King Jesus or *to observe* him accurately? Why are both needful? What resources can help you improve?
6. Why is *intentional seeing* necessary? Which of the three obstacles to intentional seeing do you struggle with the most? Why?
7. What does it mean to be Jesus's disciple? Why is general self-denial not sufficient for discipleship?
8. Name a disciple of Jesus you admire. What has it cost that person? What has being a disciple of Jesus cost you? What benefits are you gaining?

9. What does it mean to say, "the Christ is the living law"? How does Jesus's status as living law inform how disciples of Jesus should live?

10. Do you struggle more to love God or love your neighbor? What steps can you take to improve?

11. Why is Christian community—the church—essential for transformation into Jesus's image?

12. What brings about conformity to Jesus's image in a final sense? What is the connection between worship and conformity to Jesus's image?

Good News for the Nones

I am a Protestant who teaches theology in a Catholic university. It's great, but occasionally there are struggles. Sometimes the challenge is to press for the fullest biblical truths. At other times it is to remember my context. During a talk I mentioned that "nones" were on the rise in the Western world. Since religious vocations have been down for nuns, some in my audience were surprised but pleased. I had to scramble to clarify. Not that kind.

An increasing number of people do not identify at all with any religion, church, or related organization. Some "nones" are hardline atheists. But most are agnostic. They are unsure about God, gods, or religion. Many are vague I-am-spiritual-but-not-religious types who think there is probably a higher power but find themselves unwilling to commit to a specific religion. They feel science and technology provide the real solutions. Religion is perceived as irrelevant for everyday life.

High-profile deconversions have placed these nones in the cultural spotlight. Ex-evangelical celebrity pastor Joshua Harris made waves when he announced on his Instagram account that he hadn't merely kissed dating goodbye, but also Christianity: "I have undergone a massive shift in regard to my faith in Jesus. . . . By all the measurements that I have for defining a Christian, I am not a Christian."[1] He followed up his announcement by divorcing his wife, marching in a gay-rights parade, and attempting to make extra coin with a new hustle—selling kits to help others deconvert.

In our increasingly secular landscape it is trendier to dismantle traditional Christianity than to embrace it. In this environment, the church will not advance by cultural diffusion. That isn't necessarily bad. It is doubtful that true Christianity transmits appreciably that way anyway.

To attract outsiders and bolster insiders, we must be able to answer for ourselves and the world a question of singular importance: Why should a person respond to the gospel—both initially and as an ongoing commitment? Put more simply, *Why be a Christian?*

This chapter analyzes why the church is failing to attract outsiders and is losing insiders, and it offers suggestions to help reverse the trend. For each point of failure with outsiders and insiders, it gives possible correctives rooted in what Scripture says about the gospel and its purposes.

The answers that the church has been in the habit of giving about why a person should respond to the gospel are true—forgiveness, heaven, life in God's presence, freedom from sin, and growth in virtue. But because they are inadequately rooted in the gospel's deepest purposes, they are less than fully motivating. In the long run, answers that touch on the most foundational gospel aims will be the most sustaining for the church and compelling for the world.

Scripture shows us that this book's central question—*Why the gospel?*—and the most pressing question today—*Why be a Christian?*—have one and the same best answer: *because that is how honor is being restored for humans, creation, and God.* The gospel's ultimate aim also coincides with the sixth and final stage of the glory cycle: *humans reign gloriously with the King.* We find true life when we give loyalty to King Jesus, the glory restorer, and pursue his agenda.

Why Are You Not a Christian?

If you want to share with an unbelieving friend, you might broach the topic frankly: *Why are you not a Christian?* It might stir up an interesting and healthy conversation. But use caution and seek the Spirit's leading. It may prove off-putting, and a leading *why not* that non-Christians give is that Christians only want to win converts.

In truth, in our present cultural moment, outsiders have no shortage of reasons why they prefer to remain un-Christian. In a moment we'll examine a wide spectrum of reasons. But first let's briefly address a possible obstacle.

A Preliminary Concern: Slavery to Sin

We may be tempted to dismiss the reasons outsiders give for rejecting Christianity. Surely, we might conclude, those living in darkness—those shackled by worldliness, fleshly appetites, and the evil one—hate the light by virtue of their condition. Those enslaved to sin are not in a position to self-diagnose accurately. So we must turn to the Bible to discover the real reasons. Partially true. But Scripture itself suggests that this line of thought is simplistic.

Repelling and Attracting

The fuller scriptural truth is that God has given all humanity the grace of the gospel of the King—and his light simultaneously *repels and attracts everyone.* It repels everyone because it exposes the evil in which we are *all* complicit when we sin (John 3:20).

While Jesus's light repels everyone, because everyone sins, Jesus's light is also pulling everyone in, even nonbelievers. That is why Jesus exhorts the unbelieving crowds, "*Respond with fidelity [pisteuete] unto the light* while you have the light, so that you may *become children of light*" (John 12:36, AT; see also 12:46).

Jesus issued this invitation to *nonbelievers* because he knew that even those enslaved by darkness are ultimately drawn to him: "And I, when I am lifted up from the earth, will *draw all people* to myself" (John 12:31). Even nonbelievers are drawn. The "lifting up from the earth" refers to his death on the cross but also to his ascension—his return to glory at the Father's right hand (John 12:37; 17:1–5; see also John 8:28; Acts 2:33; 5:31). Once these events have transpired, the King draws *every person* to himself through his cross and enthronement. The King's light is a beacon of hope that invites *all* to switch and then maintain loyalty.

Not all choose to respond, but attraction can overcome repulsion. When non-Christians are awakened to the true light—the beauty, truth, and goodness of our King—they will no longer want to scuttle back to the darkness but will opt for Jesus and his agenda. This is why Paul, like Jesus, urges those who haven't yet responded with allegiance ("faith") to the Christ to become loyal to him. He exhorts those who are "living in disobedience" and who are surrounded by "deeds of darkness" (Eph. 5:11) to respond to the light: "Wake up, O sleeper, rise up from amid the dead—and the Christ will shine on you" (Eph. 5:14, AT). Both Jesus and Paul affirm that when nonbelievers opt to view it, the King's resurrection life is capable of rousing them. We can leave behind our deeds of darkness and step into his wonderful light.

When loyalty unites us to the King and his agenda, sin's power over us is finally broken—although it will remain an ensnaring temptation (Rom. 6:1–23; 8:1–17). Then we are free to walk with him in the light! Although sin retains a repulsive allure, the Christ's light attracts insider and outsider alike.

Striving for the Good

We are more charitable when we remember that, although non-Christians are not liberated from sin's power, most want to live a virtuous life. Because they have not submitted to God's revealed standards, they prefer to define good and evil for themselves (or to accept definitions produced by corrupt human culture). This causes harm. But that is not to say they aren't genuinely striving for virtue as they see it. For all these reasons and more, it is inappropriate—indeed rude—to assume that non-Christians opt to remain in that category simply because they want to wallow in sin.

Outsiders' Specific Obstacles

Today's outsiders have much to say about why they are *not* interested in becoming Christians. While acknowledging that sin's unbroken power affects outsiders' self-reports, we dare not dismiss them for that reason. The church should listen carefully to why outsiders find Christianity unattractive and then use Scripture to purify its reflected light.

Why are non-Christians reluctant to become Christians? Professional sociological research conducted over many years by the Barna Group indicates that non-Christians have a negative impression of Christians in six primary areas. They find Christians to be *hypocritical, too political, too focused on getting converts, antihomosexual, sheltered,* and *judgmental.*[2]

If you want to know the real obstacles—not imaginary ones—that prevent outsiders from following Jesus, then read that list again. Ponder it. Outsiders self-report that these six negatives are above all what discourages them from wanting to become Christians.

Image Problems and Gospel Purpose

A shift to a culture that prioritizes allegiance to King Jesus over trusting a savior could help realign faulty impressions in all six of these areas. To choose just one example, consider the antihomosexual charge.

When being a Christian is about allegiance first rather than the removal of guilt for wrong actions, then *everyone* must reevaluate. King Jesus requires all humans to realign their sexual appetites and practices in light of Scripture—those who self-identify as heterosexual, homosexual, bisexual, or celibate—so that they conform to his directives. When allegiance is prioritized, the accusation that the church is antihomosexual fades, since homosexuals are not singled out. Every disciple is called to deny their raw fleshly appetites and learn afresh God's standards.

But out of the six obstacles for non-Christians, the first three are especially pertinent to this book's topic. So in what follows, I'll discuss outsiders' charges that Christians are (1) *hypocritical*, (2) *too political*, and (3) *too focused on getting converts*.

And let's face it immediately. These outsiders' descriptions carry significant truth, because professing Christians frequently fail to practice what they preach, often engage in partisan politics, and frequently obsess over numeric growth. For each topic I will make suggestions for how today's church can seize on the gospel's true purposes in order to improve its image with outsiders.

Hypocrisy

Hypocrisy is the number one reason non-Christians find Christianity unattractive. Former insiders who have abandoned church also report that it is a major reason.

What is hypocrisy? It's when you say everyone should practice forgiveness, but you harbor grudges. It's when you cry out, "Be honest!" but you fudge your reported hours to get a bigger paycheck. It's when you advocate for sexual purity but secretly pursue filth. No one likes a hypocrite.

But it is time to look in the mirror. We *all* fail to live up to our ideals—non-Christians and Christians alike—more often than we'd care to admit. Due to sin, there will always be some disconnect between what we say we should do and our actual choices. The real question is, how can we minimize hypocrisy?

Through allegiance to the King.

Shifting to Royal Imagery

We can fight hypocrisy by shifting the primary image for how Jesus rescues. Replace *trusting a savior* with *giving allegiance to a king*. Both ideas are biblical. But the shape of the gospel and the meaning of our "faith" with respect to "the Christ" in Scripture indicate that loyalty to a king should be the dominant image, whereas trust in a savior should be secondary. We need to make this switch because as stand-alone ideas, trust leads more readily to hypocrisy than allegiance.

Mind and Body Reconnected

Hypocrisy happens when *what you say you believe* does not correspond with *what your body does*. Allegiance to a king better holds together mind and body than does trusting a savior for two reasons.

First, unlike trust, allegiance demands your *entire* self. Trust in Jesus for forgiveness is a mental process that requires you to submit only a small portion of your mind, and it does not automatically implicate the body. Trusting in Jesus includes at least three mental events: (1) amid many things I might think about otherwise, *attending to the relevant doctrinal content* ("God through Jesus offers forgiveness"), (2) *intellectual agreement* that the doctrine is valid ("it is true that forgiveness is found through Jesus"), and (3) a disposition of *personal reliance* ("it is true for me personally that I have been forgiven, because I have trusted in Jesus for that"). But these three mental events do not require the submission of your *entire mind* to Jesus, and they may or may not involve bodily service.

On the other hand, giving allegiance to a king implicates your mind and body entirely. Through your public confession of loyalty (*pistis*) with your mouth, ordinarily accompanied by your physical entrance into the baptismal waters, you are placing your whole self—body, mind, spirit—at your King's disposal. You have sworn to be the King's loyal servant holistically, to the best of your ability, even though you know a lifelong struggle to quell your old self's rebellion awaits you.

Allegiance includes trust but is a bigger category. Allegiance is less likely to devolve into hypocrisy than mere trust because it requires not just a select portion of your mental life, but your entire self—mind, body, and spirit.

More than a Forgiveness Dispenser

Second, allegiance addresses the most foundational salvation problem. Trust in Jesus as Savior wrongly assumes that the primary salvation problem is that we are sinners in need of forgiveness. We do need forgiveness. But Scripture indicates that the primary problem that God is trying to solve is not the erasure of human guilt per se, but rather the human failure to distribute God's glory to creation (see chapter 3).

When we mistakenly make "trust in Jesus for forgiveness" primary, then Jesus's chief function is to serve as the cosmic forgiveness machine. I am led to think that, along with the rest of the world, I have one problem: I've sinned. I need my guilt erased. So I trust Jesus. He dishes forgiveness out. I sin again. I repent. I tell Jesus that I'm still trusting him for forgiveness. He forgives. Repeat. . . . Over time it is easy to arrive at a dubious conclusion: forgiving sin is Jesus's main job, and so as long as I say "sorry" once in a while, ongoing sin is not a big deal.

Allegiance to Jesus as King puts the focus not on Jesus as the cosmic forgiveness dispenser, but on his appropriate rule over me and all others. I understand that Jesus is my King. I love him and owe him my all. He has a *mission*, *way of life*, and *tasks* for us as a group. He is inviting us toward total transformation so we can fully join him in his rule. Allegiance initializes and maintains my union with him, so it is *how* he is saving me.

When kingship is foregrounded, I'm more likely to think about allegiant obedience. I'm less likely to think about what I can get away with while still finding forgiveness. In other words, I'm less likely to be a hypocrite.

Too Political

Meet Brandon, who self-identifies as an agnostic. He describes his current experience with Christians: "Today whenever I experience the activities of American Christians as an organized group . . . it is almost always in terms of them trying to use political force to entice people to behave in a certain way."[3] It is striking that when Brandon thinks about Christian activities, what leaps to mind is not prayer, worship, love for God, concern for neighbor, charitable deeds, or affection for creation. It is political coercion.

Political Bullies

Unfortunately, Brandon is far from alone in finding political coercion to be the new face of Christianity. The Barna Group's studies showed that 48 percent of the US population is concerned about the role of conservative Christians in politics. It is one of the main reasons non-Christians give in explaining why they aren't interested in becoming Christians.[4]

Brandon's impressions are doubly striking when we discover that he is a Republican. So he favors many of the policies for which conservative American Christians agitate. Yet even still he finds that Christians today are so heavily invested in power politics that it has become their primary identity marker. If an agnostic like Brandon finds this distasteful, even though he is a political ally to conservative Christianity, imagine how left-leaning non-Christians feel.

This is not about right versus left. The issue is that *outsiders sense Christians are more committed to the left or right political camp than to Jesus.* When Christians are more known for partisan politics than their acts of mercy, it is no wonder that many non-Christians can't imagine becoming Christian. It is a major obstacle.

The True Political Gospel

But make no mistake on this point: *the gospel is political to the core.* It is also inescapably social. Those who say otherwise—I'm resisting the temptation to name prominent names here—have badly misunderstood the gospel. They've misidentified the heart of the gospel as personal reconciliation with God by mental faith rather than seeing the gospel for what it is in Scripture: the announcement that Jesus has become the King over every aspect of the universe.

We don't receive personal regeneration that awakens faith and then come to accept Jesus's kingship. That is precisely backward. When Jesus became King he provided saving benefits like regeneration and reconciliation for his people. We enter those benefits personally when we give allegiance ("faith") to Jesus as King, not before.

The announcement "Jesus is King" is at bedrock a political claim. Moreover, it is not simply an otherworldly vision, as if Jesus only has a rightful claim as King over "souls" or "hearts" rather than over all the world's political affairs and social realities. When Jesus said, "My kingdom is not *from* this world" (John 18:36), he was describing *the source* of his authority, not its scope or range. To the contrary, Scripture is clear that Jesus rules over everything, including earthly political leaders, governments, and citizens.

Because the gospel is political and has a social vision, Christians do not need to be less political. *Christians need to be more political—but in a way that aligns with their King's power-in-weakness approach.* The key is to recognize how and where Jesus's kingship is functionally operative today.

The How of Jesus's Rule

Jesus's reign over everything is presently *noncoercive*. This means his rule is always in effect but it is not forced upon people. Therefore it is not always acknowledged.

All spheres of life are under Jesus's direct sovereignty, but his present policy allows his governance to be rejected. One day "every knee will bow" (Phil. 2:10). Now many proud knees are unbent. Jesus is OK with this, and his followers must follow suit. One day "every tongue will confess 'Jesus is Lord'" (Phil. 2:11). Currently, however, many tongues loudly champion other lords and gods. Jesus permits this for the meanwhile. If Christians are to follow their King's policies, they must allow nonbelievers to hold faulty allegiances, while testifying persuasively to Jesus's ultimate kingship.

The Where of Jesus's Rule

Christians often feel that Jesus's reign is not a political option in the real world. "I can't vote for Jesus, he is not on the ballot," is a common refrain. While this is true, it also misunderstands where Jesus's real political power is operative today.

Not everyone is in rebellion. There are pockets, here and there, where he really does reign, right now. When the true church gathers, it confesses, "Jesus is the Christ!" in recognition of his authority, desire, and ability to rule his people.

If churchgoers are not confessing "Jesus is King" (explicitly or implicitly) when they worship together, then the church does not exist in that place. The church is created, maintained, and built up as initially Peter and then others confess that Jesus is the Christ (Matt. 16:16–18; Mark 8:29). Without confession of Jesus's kingship and an intention to heed his sovereign directives, a gathering is merely a Jesus admiration society with an auxiliary band. It is not the church. The church exists when two or three or more gather in Jesus's name because those who gather recognize and welcome his presence as the sovereign authority (Matt. 18:18–20; cf. 1 Cor. 5:4–5; 12:1–3). *Jesus reigns through the Holy Spirit wherever his rule is welcomed and freely obeyed, because his present policy is a noncoercive rule.*

When we declare "Jesus is the King" with integrity, we are inviting Jesus to rule over us—here and now—and are expressing our keen desire to heed his sovereign decisions. The greatest urgency and struggle on Sunday morning (and in other meetings) is to sincerely make this specific confession with a readiness to listen and obey, so that a gathering can actually *become* the church.

The church is the church only when it is the King's citizen body. Our political and social hopes are rooted in the King's community.

Political How?

Since the gospel is inherently political, it is impossible to be a Christian and be uncommitted to a political position. To be a Christian is to have accepted Jesus's political reign and his social vision—or, at least, to be in the process of learning how to do so.

Christians should be political first by submitting to Jesus's kingship as they gather with other Christians. Then they can effectively bear witness to Jesus's noncoercive, suffering-for-others, glorious reign *from within that location.*

The *how* of Jesus's politics is to allow the Holy Spirit to demonstrate his cross-and-resurrection power in the midst of our frail human weaknesses as we serve others in his name (2 Cor. 4:3–11; 13:4). Christians must be more political than they currently are by fostering an alternative political life and society in the local church that attests to the reality of Jesus's present rule in that gathered body. Jesus's reign should spill out to neighborhoods, cities, and the world from there.

Christians also should participate in politics outside the church. But their political footprint outside the church should mostly be oriented toward supporting policies that aid the vulnerable and encourage submission to Jesus's kingship within the church—while testifying that a better alternative politics extends into the world *only from that source.* When outsiders see the church, they should see that God's restorative glory truly is present and overflowing where Jesus is allowed to rule in the midst of his people—that humans, creation, and God are brought to ever higher levels of honor there.

If Christians are busier pointing right or left than they are gathering with others to confess "Jesus is King" and submit to his rule, then they've been inappropriately captured by partisan politics. When Christians fail to practice King Jesus's power-in-weakness politics, outsiders only see unholy alliances, left-versus-right hatred, and the application of a coercive ethic. When we proclaim, "Jesus is King," we have the chance to show outsiders that Jesus's reign can gloriously transform a citizen body.

Counting Converts

Beyond hypocrisy and partisan politics, non-Christians are non-plussed when Christians prioritize numeric growth through conversion. This directly stems from a gospel problem. Malformed transactional versions of the gospel generally allow a person to "count" as a convert even if that person does not seek a life of allegiance (see chapter 2).

Within a distorted gospel framework, you make your decision to trust—and that is perceived as your true moment of salvation. Who you are is irrelevant; just trust the message that "Jesus died for your sins." Now God has given Jesus your guilt and you have received his obedience so you are ready for heaven. God, robot-like, slapped a "forgiven" label on you that can never be removed. Afterward it's not horribly important if you slip into sin—right?—since you are saved. Who you are and who you are becoming matters not a bit because you have the "forgiven" sticker. Now you are forever a Christian convert, so your salvation can be tallied and reported to others.

Versions of the gospel that emphasize transaction do not follow Scripture's gospel logic and are dehumanizing. The actual gospel is about how Jesus became the Christ and sent benefits to restore his people. When you first give loyalty, there is a change in status since you really do become part of God's liberated and forgiven people through Jesus's atoning work (see chapter 4). There is a transaction in that sense. But here's the key point: *ongoing allegiance is the transformative process through which God continues saving you.* Who you are and who you are becoming—your person, character, and virtues—absolutely do matter for your final salvation. The true gospel's purpose is full recovery.

The true loyalty-demanding gospel of King Jesus changes the focus within conversion from *quantity* to *quality*. The shift is from counting the number of souls saved to the quality of restored humanity. Furthermore, this makes sense because we know how delightfully bizarre God has made each of us. We are not one-size-fits-all androids that simply need a "forgiven" sticker in order to be fully rescued by God. We have different gifts, struggles, and potentials that inform what it means for God to save each of us uniquely and maximally.

Who you are and who you are becoming—your person, character, and virtues—absolutely do matter for your final salvation.

When outsiders (and insiders) are valued in the restorative process of salvation for who they are now—and for the *quality* of person they can uniquely become—they are more likely to respond favorably to the gospel.

Failing with Insiders

We have just explored three reasons why non-Christians say they find Christianity unacceptable. I've suggested that the church's struggle with hypocrisy, power politics, and convert counting stem from a failure to adequately grasp the true gospel and its purposes. But the problem is even more severe.

Christian "insiders" are also increasingly hitting the exit ramp. Studies by the Barna Group (and others) show that young adults raised in the church are leaving it—and Jesus altogether— at an accelerated rate compared to past generations. This is an alarming trend.

In comparison with outsiders, those exiting describe the church in slightly different but equally negative ways. The studies suggest that common factors are causing disconnection among those who walk away. As with outsider reasons, we must push past our vague imaginings about why we think insiders are leaving and discover their stated reasons if we are to have any hope of correcting problems.

Previous insiders who no longer self-identify as Christians most frequently describe their upbringing and church experience in one (or several) of the following ways: *overprotective, shallow, antiscience, repressive, exclusive,* and *leaving no room for questioning or doubt.*[5] These negatives did not necessarily cause these previous insiders to leave, but they are contributing factors to the primary reasons.

In synthesizing what these young adults report, the Barna studies identify three major causes of abandonment. First, those in this new generation are jettisoning Christianity because they are not finding authentic relationships through church—gatherings are superficial and not sufficiently cross-generational. Second, the church is a source of simplistic information, but not of the wisdom that comes through wrestling with the complexities, difficulties, and doubts that attend Christianity. Third, the church does not impart a holistic vocation—church life is compartmentalized and has no relevance to career.[6]

In sum, due to an overarching discipleship failure, young adults report that they are leaving the church because they are not finding (1) *authentic relationships,* (2) *wisdom in dealing with doubts and complexities,* and (3) a *holistic vocation.* Let's begin with the larger issue of discipleship as a whole and then address each.

The Basic Discipleship Failure

They were forgiven by God once for all time as they approached the foot of the cross. They had been born again into eternal life. They now had God's unshakable promise of heaven. Or so they were taught. If a culture that prioritized "counting converts" has proven highly off-putting to outsiders, it has gutted insiders.

What has gone wrong? Self-reports show a macro problem: most of these insiders were never personally taught how to be disciples of

Jesus by other Christians. Disciple-making wasn't a priority in the church cultures they inhabited.

It's not hard to see why this discipleship failure is happening. It is a gospel fiasco. If pastors and elders are convinced—and persuade those under their care—that all the real work of salvation happens when an individual first trusts the gospel of Jesus's forgiveness, then why prioritize discipleship? Spend all your effort instead trying to get your friends and neighbors to pray that sinner's prayer.

Allegiance Plus Time

The truth about conversion is different once we recognize that the gospel is about Jesus's saving kingship followed by our allegiance (faith) response *over the course of time.* As such, initial decisions to follow King Jesus remain exciting. They still very much count! But they count in the sense of *matter,* not in the sense of filling a quota.

A person is saved by nothing more or less than allegiance to King Jesus—past, present, and future. When you first declared allegiance—ordinarily at your baptism—you were "saved." That is, you got "saved," because you genuinely entered the Spirit-filled community that has right standing with God and is in the process of being saved.

But salvation is a journey. We must continue to give loyalty to King Jesus. It is a learning process. Our allegiance will be mixed, half-hearted, and compromised. Failures, mistakes, and acts of treason against the King are inevitable for individuals and for the church. We must have a posture of ongoing repentance for our imperfect loyalty.

Our imperfect allegiance ("faith") is sufficient to unite us to our perfect King's righteousness, forgiveness, and life-giving power. We are part of the imperfect body of the King, but we are made perfect by our royal head. Yet for this union to be present, an overall trajectory and intention of loyalty to our King must remain intact. The lifelong pursuit of and disposition toward allegiance are in the end all that count for salvation.

In other words—as nearly all Christians down through the ages have affirmed—we must persevere in our confession of faith in order to reach final salvation. If a person ceases to give allegiance to the Christ *entirely*—abandons any attempt to render faith unto the Christ—that person is no longer part of the saved community because they have rejected the gospel (1 Cor. 15:2; 1 Tim. 1:19–20; Heb. 3:12–14; 6:4–6).

We submit to the King's authority by undertaking a life of discipleship. We have already discussed how to *come* and *see*, in order to become a disciple (see chapter 5). Since we are saved by allegiance ("faith") to King Jesus past, present, and future, then there is no separation between salvation and discipleship. The path of allegiance to King Jesus is the path of transformative discipleship.

What about the Thief?

By this stage of the book, I hope you've been persuaded that the proper full response to the gospel is bodily allegiance or loyal discipleship—and are pondering implementation. (If not, I'd encourage you to read the more scholarly treatments that I and others have written.[7]) But there is a possible counterexample that is so famous that it needs to be discussed. Nearly every time I teach this material publicly, I am asked how to handle it.

What about the thief who was crucified alongside Jesus?[8] Wasn't he saved solely by trusting in Jesus's death? After all, the thief had no opportunity for discipleship, yet Jesus said to him, "Today you will be with me in paradise" (Luke 23:43). Doesn't that prove that neither loyalty nor discipleship is necessary, but rather the true criterion must be mental trust in Jesus's death?

The thief is not a valid counterexample. This becomes obvious if we pay attention to what the thief *actually said (rather than what we think he ought to have said)* and are attuned to a kingdom gospel. The thief acknowledges his sinful deeds, just desserts, and Jesus's innocence, but he does *not* say, "Jesus, I'm trusting that your death covers my sins." On the contrary, he says, "Jesus, remember me when you come into *your kingdom*" (Luke 23:42). The thief is not described as trusting solely in Jesus's death but instead asserts that Jesus will reign over a kingdom.

The thief makes the quintessential gospel confession. He acknowledges that Jesus's claim to be the Christ is true. While watching Jesus die, the thief expresses faith that in a future era God will install Jesus as the sovereign. This is a public confession of personal allegiance—the thief asks Jesus to *remember him*—showing his future willingness to appear before King Jesus in acknowledgment of his rule. The thief displays confidence that King Jesus will have the authority to bestow benefits to him personally. It is the thief's public confession of Jesus's sovereignty that prompts Jesus to announce this man's rescue. The thief is saved because he acknowledges Jesus as the coming King.

Vampire Christians?

The true gospel does not permit Vampire Christians, as Dallas Willard so memorably called that monstrosity.[9] Vampire Christians are those who want to make use of Jesus's blood but have no interest in genuinely acknowledging him as Lord. To call them Vampire *Christians* is in fact inaccurate—as I'm sure Willard would agree. They are merely vampires.

If those vampires who want Jesus's blood apart from allegiant discipleship falsely claim the Christian name, Jesus will tell them plainly, "I never knew you. Depart from me you evildoers" (Matt. 7:23). Since salvation is by allegiance to King Jesus alone, it is not possible to "get saved" by believing or trusting in Jesus's blood while having no intention to submit to his authority by becoming his disciple.

The church can best meet the decline among insiders by— surprise!—preaching and teaching the true gospel of King Jesus. The true gospel addresses the church's discipleship failure because it helps the church shift its energy from evangelism to disciple-making, for they are no longer a different task. To respond to the gospel in a saving fashion is nothing more or less than to commit to becoming a loyal disciple of King Jesus.

Let's see how the true gospel addresses three specific problems that are causing former insiders to reject Christianity.

Lack of Authentic Relationships

It is sadly ironic. Because even though this generation has unparalleled access to connective technology there is a black hole surrounding meaningful interpersonal relationships. Beyond hypocrisy and obsession with conversion, one of the most frequently cited reasons for abandoning church—and often Christianity—is *relational alienation.*[10]

Bowling alone indeed. Except, heightening the isolation, now people are more likely to bowl alone on their phone than with a real ball in a public venue. The institutional church, it is felt, promises healthy meaningful relationships but fails to deliver.

Disciple-Making Is Relational

The church struggles to foster deep relationships through its standard "Let's present the gospel to the masses" programming. Mentally trusting Jesus for forgiveness is what truly matters in the standard gospel presentation, not placing your body in the presence of a more experienced disciple's body so that together you try to better practice allegiant obedience to your King.

If we are to recapture Jesus's disciple-making mission, what it means to respond to the gospel must change in our local churches. Since disciple-making involves coming and seeing—entering into another's pattern of life to pursue King Jesus together—it is an inherently *relational* activity. Because it is intrinsically interpersonal, intentional disciple-making is key to overcoming relational alienation.

It's not just any relationships, but intergenerational relationships that manifest the entire body of the King that are needful in today's church. Yet "these connections won't happen by accident," as David Kinnaman helpfully reminds us. "Deep relationship happens only by spending time, large chunks of it, in shared experiences."[11] So it will be necessary to deprogram or reprogram in order to make ample space for disciple-making.

Reprogramming for Disciple-Making

This does not mean that churches should abandon formal programming. Shepherds of the church cannot count on spontaneous gatherings. Even when informal gatherings happen among Christians, they may not be with an intention toward disciple-making.

I once knew a pastor who was fond of saying, "let's just do life together." But he seemed to spend far more time talking about alcohol than Jesus. Don't misunderstand. I enjoy alcohol in moderation. But, please, recognize: "let's just do life together" only works as a pastoral slogan if those involved intend more than drinking bouts. It only works if they are seriously and consistently committed to trying to be more like Jesus as they "do life." Programming and events are necessary. However, they must foster not merely shared experiences, but ample space for intentional disciple-making.

Are you interested in becoming a disciple-maker? Find a group of three to twelve who are willing to walk alongside you in order to learn together how to better practice Jesus's ways. Meet for that purpose regularly in structured and nonstructured ways. There are outstanding tools to help you get started.[12]

Lack of Wisdom

Life's complexities and uncertainties assail outsider and insider alike. Christianity offers a comprehensive explanation of reality. It is a metanarrative, a master story that seeks to explain everything in the universe. It tells us why God's universe is orderly yet surprising, what it means to be human, and how we should behave.

But Christianity is not the only metanarrative on offer today. Alternative worldviews purport to explain reality in even more convincing ways. Apart from other world religions, Christianity's main competitor is atheistic materialism—also called scientific naturalism or secular humanism.

Insiders, even when they remain Christian, feel pressured by these alternatives. *How certain am I that Christianity is true?* they ask. Youths and young adults raised in the church feel it most acutely because they begin life with a Christian worldview and are only gradually exposed to the best arguments for alternatives. If they are to remain Christian, they have no choice except to persevere in faith-seeking-understanding while they wrestle with doubts.

Knowing alternative worldviews pose a threat, pastors and parents wisely shield the young. Children aren't ready for Foucault, Ehrman, or Dawkins. Well, maybe they are ready for Dawkins, since his arguments are rather juvenile, but the point is we should discern what is age-appropriate. All too often, however, due to fear, ignorance, or both, the church overshelters.

It is no surprise that insiders who abandon Christianity frequently report that they were overly sheltered. Church leaders must come to grips with the present crisis: simplistic one-sided information won't cut it for young adults who can find details and counterevidence through a simple Google search—and they can do it in the middle of your sermon or talk.

Mitch's story is not unusual. While undertaking medical training, his faith reached a crisis point. When he was first exposed to evolutionary theory in a serious way—and increasingly found it convincing—he tried to reconcile it with Christianity. But he found himself unable. "When I read through the evidence on evolution, I wondered at what point was the soul imparted? Did God come down and touch a prehuman hominid with a soul?"[13] As he wrangled with such questions as part of his training, he felt he was forced to choose between Christianity and his vocation in the sciences. Ultimately he abandoned Christianity.

Curating Information for Wisdom

Mitch is not alone. The modern world continues to hit Christians with stiff intellectual challenges. But would Mitch have left if his pastor had pointed him to resources produced by our ablest Christian researchers? Maybe. But maybe not.

Christianity continues to be well defended by brilliant scientists, philosophers, and historians. Sometimes they even team up. For example, Christian evolutionary biologist Dennis Venema and renowned biblical scholar Scot McKnight bring readers up to speed on the latest developments in their *Adam and the Genome*.[14] Church leaders need to lean on the expertise of trusted Christian academics and resourcing networks to help those under their care to locate *curated resources* that will frame and interpret intellectual challenges, so those wrestling can ultimately develop a robust Christian wisdom.

The most pressing challenges many insiders face are not intellectual but moral. Since Christianity is rooted in ancient history, followers wonder to what degree its ethical vision still applies today. For example, since the Bible tells women not to braid their hair or wear jewelry, should I avoid these things today? The Bible forbids adultery, but that involves infidelity for married people, so does Scripture forbid all sexual activities outside of marriage?

Most mature disciples of Jesus discern that the answer to the first question is no and the second yes. But it is not enough to appeal to authority or tradition in our current moral environment. Insiders who have been burdened—and burned—by petty legalism in the past need to be taught how to arrive at such answers themselves. They need to know *how* and *why* Christianity offers not just ancient information, but today's *wisdom*.

Good News for Doubters

What happens when a person, like Mitch, who has trusted in Jesus for personal forgiveness finds that they have overwhelming doubts? What if they want to believe but find that on certain days or for a season, they can't get over an intellectual hurdle? Are they still a Christian? Being a Christian does involve intellectually affirming the truthfulness of the actual gospel's content (see chapter 4). But *how certain* about its truthfulness does a person have to be?

Mitch felt forced to choose. I don't know what version of the gospel he heard. But I do know that deficient ways of presenting the gospel create unnecessary obstacles and make the hurdle higher than it needs to be.

When my wife was a teenager, one of her pastors told the congregation—from the pulpit on a Sunday morning—that he had just become a Christian. Previously he had thought that he was trusting Jesus's forgiveness. Lately, however, he had come to realize that he wasn't fully trusting but was still clinging to his "works"—his status and achievements as a minister. Now, he was happy to report that he had become a Christian, because he was really resting fully in Jesus for forgiveness.

The congregation was surprised to discover that their pastor had not in fact been a Christian. But whatever his struggles, they rejoiced that he had now responded wholeheartedly. They were less thrilled several months later when he told them that he had once again become a Christian. He and the church parted ways shortly thereafter. But not before he converted a third time!

This sincere pastor was also sincerely confused about the gospel and saving faith. I'm not saved by trusting—I mean *really* trusting with all my might and main—that my trust in Jesus is effective. Nor is the true gospel about whether or not I am trusting Jesus's righteousness alone rather than my works.[15] Such a construal, which is usually based on a misreading of Paul, puts far too much *me* and *my* in the gospel. Me—with all my doubts. Plus trying really hard to make yourself believe something can involve not just mental gymnastics, but impossible contortion.

Saving faith is not aimed in the first instance at personal atonement or the justification process. It is aimed at the enthroned Christ. Then those benefits follow. What matters is my overall intention to stay on or get back on the path of allegiance despite whatever sinful disloyalty might derail me.

Less than Certain

Nor is a *total lack of doubt* pertinent. When a doubter has become convinced that salvation depends upon the ability to truly trust, anxiety builds. The purportedly good news that the only needful thing is *really* to trust becomes a devastating word of condemnation.

The faulty God-only-accepts-my-genuine-trust gospel puts doubters in a tailspin, but the true gospel of Jesus's kingship gives a clear answer regarding salvation's boundary: *if a doubter continues to give allegiance to Jesus—the King revealed in the gospel—then that person is saved despite whatever doubts they harbor.* Even on his or her most doubt-filled days, the doubter can still choose to give loyalty to King Jesus and his ways.

The vast majority of contemporary Christians struggle with doubt. I know I'm not immune. Churches should encourage doubters by reminding them that they can and should be intellectually adventurous—all truths are God's truths—while championing the necessity of remaining allegiant in the midst of doubts. If doubters believe enough that their life intention is to remain loyal to the King Jesus described in the gospel, they remain on the road to salvation—even if they can't presently believe that themselves.

Making Doubts an Opportunity

Churches can use doubts as an opportunity for insiders to grow by creating reading and discussion groups where honest wrestling with the big questions is encouraged. Within an allegiance framework, because such soundings are less threatening to personal salvation, folks typically feel more leeway to explore. Evolution? Free will? Creation ex nihilo? Atonement theories? Capital punishment? Bring on the debate.

Although other rules can be added (such as those pertaining to privacy and respect), to my mind such explorative groups need have only one hard-and-fast criterion for membership: to seek to remain allegiant to King Jesus and his ways as revealed in Scripture (while recognizing that the interpretation of Scripture is a complex art and science), or to leave the group voluntarily. Since those who confess Jesus as King are led by the Holy Spirit, such groups may suffer confusing setbacks and wander through perilous waters, but they ultimately will be led into deeper truths.

Lack of Holistic Vocation

The gospel of King Jesus can facilitate wisdom with regard to intellectual and moral challenges. It also helps with a related issue—nurturing an integrated life. With a faulty gospel in place, vocation is bifurcated rather than holistic, causing Christians to wander away from the church.

Consider Eugene's disconnected experience. He is a Christian but works as a journalist for major newspapers. "In the newsroom, I am constantly trying to help my editors tell accurate stories about religion and faith communities." The newsroom's editors are not sympathetic to Eugene's distinctively Christian concerns. Yet outside the office Eugene has Christians barking at him for even opting for such a career. They "can't understand why I would work here or why I would work in media at all."[16]

A distorted gospel contributes to a split personality—a vocational fracture—among Christians: Dr. Jekyll is the churchgoer, Mr. Hyde the worker. If forgiveness, heaven, or God's glory alone is the endgame toward which the gospel aims, then work and church are more readily compartmentalized into the secular and sacred. You work for five or six days a week in one world, but on Sunday you enter another. The two scarcely intersect. So it is hard to be the same person in each.

Moreover, within a faulty gospel framework, work is not meaningful in its own right. My vocation and my labor become significant only if they present an opportunity to share the gospel with a lost soul. Eugene's remarks about church read like a wistful lament: "It was really hard finding a church where I could learn about how to be a good Christian in the middle of this tension."

The Gospel and Work's Glory

The King Jesus gospel better integrates vocation and work into the Christian life. When we recognize that the one true gospel's endgame is restoration within image-bearing so that God's glory can reach creation and other humans *through our work*, then our labor is not just a means toward an end. Work comes to have dignity in its own right.

Our work can be a new-creation signpost. A trucker's work is not meaningful only if she can share the gospel with another trucker at a rest stop. It is meaningful because truckers serve and steward by distributing resources and goods in a way that allows civilization to flourish in an orderly fashion. A clerk's work is not significant only if he manages to slip a reference to Jesus into a conversation. It is glorious when he serves customers and safeguards transactions in a way that allows others to thrive. Likewise, Eugene's work is meaningful when he continues to report on religion with excellence and integrity. It is how he makes God's glory touch where it otherwise would not reach. Each of these helps humanity develop from the untamed garden to the cultivated city—the new Jerusalem—where God will dwell directly in the midst of his people (see Rev. 21–22).

Right now creation, and our work within it, is tainted by our broken personal, social, and cosmic sinfulness. So creation groans. It longs for the freedom that it will experience when *the glory* of the children of God fully reaches it (Rom. 8:21). But—good news!—healing is in process right now.

We only experience creation's mending in fits and starts in our work at present. But it is enough to know that recovery is underway. The transformation of our image—and the recovery of the glory that attends that transformation—fulfills the gospel's purpose, as those among all nations practice loyal obedience. Each Christian's diverse and unique work is an opportunity to exercise the restorative stewardship God intends for his whole creation.

Stage 6: Reigning Gloriously with the King

In this way the glory cycle that we've traced in this book is completed (for a review, see p. 57). In the end we become like Jesus to such a degree that our labor distributes God's glory to other humans and to creation in a Jesus-shaped way. When we carry out our work in

Jesus's cross-and-resurrection–shaped fashion in the locations where we have influence, we are entering into our final Christian destiny.

God gave humans an original glory that derives from his own glory in order to distribute it to creation through human rule. In chapters 3–5 we traced that glory's devolution and recovery. But in the end, God's intention is that we *exceed* humanity's original glory. The Christ to whom we come to be conformed is more glorious than Adam. Those conformed to the Christ's image distribute his greater-than-Adam glory as they exercise stewardship over creation through their labor.

Recharged in glory by worshiping in the very presence of God, our final Christian destiny is to reign as queens and kings as local stewards of creation under the banner of Jesus the King of kings. In those rare yet special moments when we enter into that kind of work now—when we know we are doing what we were made to do—our hearts sing in delight, praise, and worship.

The world's pathetic distortion of heaven makes it a place of disembodied pleasurable ease. Heaven is best considered a waiting stage prior to the resurrection age. The final Christian vision for the future features a reinvigorated creation populated by resurrected humans. These humans, changed to be like Jesus, delight because they are performing meaningful work with their transformed bodies—work that brings glory to humans, creation, and above all to God.

The gospel is *still* good news for nones. It has rescuing power. Some nones have only ever heard the gospel in a tainted, watery form. They need stronger medicine—the pure allegiance-demanding gospel of King Jesus.

Benjamin was raised in a church but abandoned Christianity when he discovered a gross instance of hypocrisy.[17] His pastor had embezzled, bought luxury items, purchased illegal drugs, and committed adultery. This caused him to weigh his church in its entirety:

"I liked Jesus," he reports, but "His people were moral Nazis, and they had really strange rules." He gave up following Jesus.

Later Benjamin met two tattooed, beer-swigging Christians. These men spoke differently about Jesus and the world. "What won me over," Benjamin explains, "was the way they loved me and loved people who were hurting and messy. It was the way they shared openly about their hurts and repeated failures." They never asked Benjamin to pray a sinner's prayer. These men told him that Jesus's costs were higher—Benjamin's entire *life*, not just his heart. Today Benjamin is a Christian again. He is a pastor who proclaims not just a Savior, but a King.

QUESTIONS FOR DISCUSSION OR REFLECTION

1. Think of a non-Christian acquaintance. What reasons do you think he or she would give if you were to ask, *Why are you not a Christian?* What risks and rewards attend a direct approach to evangelism?

2. Outsiders give six primary reasons why they are not Christians. Which of the six seems to be the most weighty for the non-Christians you know personally? How can you and others help change non-Christian impressions?

3. Why is hypocrisy such a turnoff? In what areas of your life do you struggle the most to do what you say that you believe? Why? How can the true gospel help reduce your hypocrisy?

4. The author claims the gospel is "political to the core." How should this claim be further unpacked to add clarity and avoid misunderstanding? If previously you've thought the gospel to be apolitical, how might the recognition that it is political change your evangelism?

5. When you gather with other Christians currently, to what degree are folks making an effort to heed and obey King Jesus

during the meeting? What practical steps can you take, so that you and others are encouraged do this more when you gather?

6. How can and should a Christian be political? How can a Christian advocate for policies that will allow society as a whole to thrive while not forcing non-Christians to accept a Christian ethic?

7. Tell about someone you know who once followed Jesus but who has now stopped. Did this person give reasons for the change? Are there reasons you suspect were a factor beyond any this person gave?

8. Former insiders often report one of six factors were present in their story. These six are not always causes for leaving Christianity, but nevertheless there is a high correlation between these factors and abandonment. Which two of the six do you think are the most weighty factors? Why?

9. Sociological studies suggest that there are three major causes of abandonment for former insiders. Which of the three have you wrestled with personally the most? What has helped you persevere?

10. Why might the gospel of *King* Jesus, proclaimed alongside an *allegiance* framework, be especially good news for doubters? How can we make doubt an opportunity?

11. How does work or labor relate to human purpose and to glory?

12. What steps can you take to plant signposts that point to new creation within the midst of the grind of your daily tasks? How can you encourage a coworker to do the same?

Gospeling Backward with Purpose

"You were fantastic this season! Everyone here is a winner!" the emcee yelled. "Repeat after me: 'We are all winners!'" Some eight hundred elementary schoolkids shouted it, parroting the emcee. "Now say, 'I am awesome!'"

It was awards night to celebrate a youth basketball league. A large church was hosting the league for community outreach. This was the grand finale.

Not quite yet. The lights dimmed. A young adult was spotlighted for a gutsy five-minute Christian testimony. Then lights blazed again.

Noise and festivity returned. Perched ten feet in the air on unicycles, jugglers tossed balls ever higher. Kids, parents, and grandparents—about two thousand total—roared with delight. The emcee enthused again, "Repeat after me, 'I am a winner!'" Like obedient robots, the kids cheered it.

Seamlessly, the emcee transitioned: "Now say, 'Jesus, I know that I am a sinner, and I ask for your forgiveness. I believe you died for my sins and rose from the dead. I turn from my sins and invite you to come into my heart and life.'" The kids mouthed the words.

Then . . . immediately, door prizes! New video game systems— and other delights. Cards were passed to the kids. To enter to win, each child was required to write his or her name at the top. Below that, they were told to check one of three boxes:

☐ I accepted Jesus tonight and became a Christian!
☐ I rededicated my life to Jesus tonight!
☐ I am a Christian already.

Those were the only options.

Not a lot of wiggle room.

The kids were confused but needed to check a box to win. Some asked their parents what to write. Others turned to their mentors: "Coach, what box should I mark?" Coaches could be heard saying, "It doesn't matter, just check one of them."

The coaches were absolutely correct. They were better theologians than the event's organizers. When the gospel and salvation have been that severely misunderstood, does it really matter which box you tick?

Unfortunately, this is not a fictional story. As I pen this, I am describing an event that happened last night in a respected church in a midsize US city. My sister-in-law sent me a video clip. So I can testify that at least the jugglers on unicycles were impressive.

Despite the good intentions of the organizers, the damage done through this type of evangelism is real. Yes, when reports are filed, the number of commitments and rededications will excite trustees and donors.

But in reality such efforts undermine Jesus's kingdom. The true gospel is missing entirely. Confusion is introduced regarding the genuine process and boundaries of Christian salvation among children and adults alike. It reinforces the impression that Christians are intellectually naive and are only interested in counting converts. The previous chapter demonstrated that this style of evangelism encourages those who "made a decision" (insiders) and those who did not (outsiders) to turn away from Christianity subsequently.

If the church's mission is to be effective today, we must proclaim the true gospel and its genuine purposes rather than half-baked imitations. By and large the church has been invested in inaccurate versions of the gospel for more than a century.

By breaking down a typical gospel presentation into smaller elements, we will see why the usual pattern of presentation does not follow Scripture's logic. If we want to follow the Bible's lead with regard to the gospel, we must reverse how we present the gospel's content, decision point, individualization, and primary purposes. In other words, if the typical pattern of "how to present the gospel" is our reference point, we must learn to gospel backward.

Reversing Our Gospel Invitation

We want to proclaim the good news to others. We desire to become more rooted in the gospel ourselves. How can we do this effectively? I don't pretend to have the definitive answer. The most important task is simply to proclaim allegiance to King Jesus, whenever and however we can. But here I offer a few final reflections.

Reversing the Content

To gospel backward means to reverse the logic of the church's ordinary way of presenting the good news. The content of the gospel today in most churches is about finding forgiveness through Jesus as Savior. Jesus's kingship only comes later, if at all. To stay true to Scripture's gospel logic, we must flip the order.

> *Incorrectly ordered content*: Because he offers you forgiveness, Jesus is your <u>Savior</u>. Accept his salvation. Next he wants to be King of your life.

> *Reverse it!*

Correctly ordered content: Jesus is the King. Accept his kingship, because through it Jesus is offering you saving rescue, including the forgiveness of your sins.

Why must we present Jesus as King first? Not only because "Jesus is the Christ" best summarizes the gospel in Scripture, but also because Jesus's saving benefits, like forgiveness, are *only available through his kingship*.

The cross is of utmost importance as part of the gospel. But it is not the whole gospel. Reversing the order of the content so that King appears before Savior helps us avoid reducing the gospel to a forgiveness transaction at the cross. Jesus's incarnation, crucifixion, resurrection, enthronement, and Spirit-sending are all essential to the gospel. In his final return, King Jesus will bring the saving benefits associated with all of these to a fullness.

Re-aiming the Decision Point

Not only must we reverse the order and expand to include the whole of the gospel's content, but we must also re-aim the decision point. In Scripture, when the gospel is presented, those who hear it are encouraged to respond by repenting, pledging faith, and undertaking baptism (see Acts 2:38; 3:19; 19:4–5). It should be no different today. But the aim of "faith" and purpose of baptism within that decision point have all too often been slightly mistargeted.

Once we realize the gospel's basic content is the arrival of the kingdom of God through Jesus's attainment of cosmic kingship, it becomes obvious that "faith" is not restricted to mental trust in Jesus's atonement but involves swearing bodily loyalty to him as King. A decision point that focuses on believing in (or trusting in) Jesus for forgiveness is too narrow—it is not a response to the gospel—unless it also yields to his sovereignty. We must re-aim today by asking people to swear loyalty instead of merely asking them to trust.

Misaimed decision point: Repent, <u>trust</u> in Jesus as Savior, and then <u>receive baptism.</u>

Re-aim it!

Targeted decision point: Repent and <u>give allegiance</u> to Jesus as King <u>through baptism.</u>

There has been no small confusion in the church over how and why repentance, faith, and baptism constitute a saving response to the gospel in Scripture. Here is the truth of the matter from a New Testament perspective: A person enters salvation when they reject ungodly agendas and practices (repent) by professing loyalty (faith) to Jesus as the Christ. Although there are exceptions, ordinarily this happens definitively for the first time when a person chooses to be baptized in water—at which time they receive the Holy Spirit, because they are entering the Spirit-filled community.[1]

Originally in the New Testament "immersion" or "being dipped" (*baptisma*) included a washing and an oath of allegiance to King Jesus, so baptism was a bodily expression of repentance and faith. Baptism, for example, was "into the name of Jesus the Christ" (Acts 2:38) or "in the name of the Lord Jesus" (Acts 19:5). In fact, ultimately baptism and other rites came to be called "sacraments" as church history developed due in part to the baptismal loyalty *oath* (Latin: *sacramentum*). Baptism in the earliest church expressed allegiance to King Jesus.

Upon further scriptural analysis, we discover this meant that *the person who was being baptized* (not necessarily the person performing the baptism) was to *call upon the name of the Lord* as part of the oath-taking within the baptismal process. That is, in earliest Christianity the person who was being baptized undertook an oath of loyalty to King Jesus as part of the baptism. For instance, after the resurrected Lord Jesus appeared to Paul, he was told to be baptized by "calling on his [the Lord Jesus's] name" (Acts 22:16).[2] Paul himself, not the person baptizing Paul, was instructed to undertake an oath to his new Lord as part of his baptism. Best practices suggest we should do the same today. Rather than simply allowing a pastor or priest to speak words over us, we should swear loyalty to King Jesus when we are baptized.

We "repent" (*metanoia*) from our sins by turning away from ungodly loyalties and agendas and swearing fealty to King Jesus instead. Meanwhile, "faith" or "belief" (*pistis*) in the New Testament

---

We should swear loyalty to King Jesus when we are baptized.

---

can also mean faithfulness, loyalty, and allegiance. So when the New Testament affirms that we are saved by faith, we must recognize that not just trust in Jesus's saving work is in view, but also a commitment to give bodily allegiance to him as King.

When presenting the gospel, we should call ourselves and others toward a specific decision that matches the gospel's purpose: *allegiance to King Jesus*. We should urge all to respond to Jesus's kingship by embodying allegiance—initially through a baptismal commitment and then continuing by an ongoing repentance from other loyalties.

Reprioritizing Individual and Group

Current evangelism prioritizes individual salvation rather than group. This creates loners who falsely think the church is an optional extra beyond what an individual needs for salvation. However, in Scripture the gospel creates a saved group at Pentecost within history first; individuals enter it second. Individuals can only be saved (or "justified") by opting to join the group that, because its members have already responded to the King, enjoys that saved status.

We must reprioritize, because the true gospel invites individuals to join the team that is in the process of being rescued.

The loner gospel: You need to trust Jesus as Savior <u>so you can re-</u> <u>ceive personal forgiveness.</u> Then you will be <u>free</u> to follow Jesus as Lord—and you should find a church to help you do that.

Reprioritize it!

The join-the-team gospel: You need to declare loyalty to King Jesus, who has given saving benefits to his people, <u>so you can join</u> <u>this forgiven and free group.</u>

When we get the logic of the gospel decision backward, we think that trust in Jesus as Savior sets the individual free to pursue Jesus as Lord—and the church becomes a supplemental, optional aid to the individual in that quest. We can correct this by reversing how we gospel, so that the salvation of the King's people is emphasized before the individual.

Recalibrating the Gospel's Main Purpose

Heaven is a brief yet delightful stopover in light of eternity. Our final destiny as humans is not heaven, but resurrection into a radically renewed creation. When we expand beyond content and decision point, while taking into account group concerns, we also need to fine-tune how we speak about the gospel's purposes.

Imprecise gospel purpose: You need to trust Jesus <u>so you can be</u> <u>with God forever in heaven when you die.</u>

Recalibrate it!

Precise gospel purpose: You need to declare loyalty to King Jesus and then continue to do this, so you can participate <u>forever</u> in how he is bringing saving benefits that <u>restore glory for humans,</u> <u>creation, and God.</u>

Remember, God's love is the ultimate motive when we ask, *Why the gospel?* But the most explicit answer to the question of gospel purpose in Scripture is *loyal obedience to King Jesus in all the nations* (Rom. 1:5; 16:26). It is no coincidence that fidelity to the King is the required saving response to the gospel also.

The gospel's purpose and our required response are identical: allegiance to King Jesus. But the glory cycle helps us to see that allegiance to King Jesus is not primarily about getting into heaven. It is about the even grander "new heaven and new earth" plan of God (Rev. 21:1). It is ultimately aimed at the restoration of honor for humans, creation, and God.

Reversing a Full Gospel Presentation

In comparison with how the gospel is typically presented today, what does it mean to gospel backward completely? When we've reconfigured all that we've discussed above—the gospel's content, decision point, individualization, and purposes—then we can combine them to offer a full gospel invitation in reverse.

An inadeduate (but typical) full gospel invitation: Jesus died for your sins. Trust in Jesus as Savior for personal forgiveness. Then you'll be saved and get to go to heaven. You'll also be set free so you can be his disciple and submit to his kingship. Once you trust, you'll be saved no matter what. But you should get baptized and join a church, so you can be a better follower of Jesus.

Reverse it!

A better full gospel invitation: Jesus is now King! He offers saving benefits to all his people through his incarnation, death for sins, resurrection, enthronement, Spirit-sending, and return. If you will turn away from your other loyalties and instead swear allegiance to him through baptism as part of your commitment to be his disciple, you'll become part of his forgiven and set-free family. Our mission under King Jesus is to become like him so we can work together to restore honor to humans, creation, and God now and forever more. All of this maximizes God's glory.

Please reread the "inadequate" versus the "better" gospel invitations above with care. Ponder them. The differences are subtle but vitally important. I'd encourage you to internalize the better presentation, perhaps even to memorize it. Much of this book's practical equipping is consolidated in that comparison.

I opened this chapter with a story of an inept attempt to share the gospel at a youth basketball event. Doubtless you intuitively sensed much was wrong with it, since it was inappropriately coercive and disrespectful to non-Christians. But hopefully this section has exposed the underlying *theological* problems. That presentation followed the basic pattern in the "inadequate" example above—although it was so egregiously bad that it only focused on trusting Jesus as Savior for forgiveness and never even made a call for discipleship.

The actual gospel—that is, the one found in Scripture—reverses the logic of the typical presentation of today by emphasizing the reality of Jesus's kingship first, and second how allegiance brings about saving restoration. When we grasp and internalize the logic of the actual gospel, we are prepared to bear witness to King Jesus effectively today.

It should be understood that in suggesting this "better" gospel invitation, I am primarily interested in conveying the gospel's logic. I've reduced it to bare essentials in an attempt to expose it. In one way or another, I submit, the underlying logic of this better invitation needs to guide our evangelism. But, of course, an actual gospel presentation need not follow this exact pattern or use these words in a servile fashion. It should be far more personal, arousing, and beautiful.

Tarnished Beauty

The basic way the church must learn to gospel backward has just been sketched. But there is a quite different way to gospel in reverse. This book has asked, *Why the gospel?* If the key answer is *because allegiance to King Jesus is what restores honor*, then the church will thrive when restoration receives priority.

Please do not consider what I say next prescriptive. We share the gospel effectively when we testify to Jesus's kingship. Period. It's more important simply to do *that*—whenever and however we are led—than to obsess about technique. There is no silver bullet of evangelism.

It is vital to follow Scripture's gospel logic by presenting the reality of Jesus's kingship first. But beyond that, what it means to best testify to Jesus has a million forms spoken with a billion tongues into countless different lives. What is best for each hearer will vary, because it depends on unique circumstances. Let the Spirit lead.

The Problem of Personal Plight

But I do think certain patterns of gospel presentation are less and more effective. For example, it is usually less effective today to start with personal plight—to warn that the unsaved individual is unrighteous due to sin and under God's judgment. Despite its truth, this is usually an unwise place to start for three reasons.

First, since most unbelievers are skeptical about the final judgment and God's willingness to punish—and do not necessarily believe the Bible—hellfire warnings do little to persuade.

Second, such warnings are especially ineffective among hearers who see glimpses of startling beauty in the midst of creation's brokenness. Doubly so if these hearers have been told repeatedly that they are hopeless sinners, but if they only mentally trust Jesus as Savior then everything will be OK personally—but that all the rest of the loveliness within God's gorgeous creation is bound for the fire. A truer biblical image for the final outcome for creation is a melting connected to refinement followed by a recovery based on God's new creation work (for example, 1 Cor. 3:11–15; Heb. 10:26–29; 2 Pet. 3:10–13; Rev. 20:7–21:2).Warnings of judgmental destruction don't jive with those attuned to God's beauty.

Third, and most vitally, dire warnings of personal punishment after death rankle because they don't *first* speak truly about God's motives in giving the gospel. Those who have been browbeaten by theologies that overemphasize worthlessness especially need to hear the good news of God's love before being hit with the bad news of condemnation.

Although personal warning has a valid place in evangelism, it is not normally a good starting point. I think this is true even though I agree that eternal personal rescue from death and punishment is an enormously important benefit of the gospel. It is wiser to give God's basic purposes in giving the gospel front billing in our evangelism: *God loves humans and his creation, and he wants to restore both.*

God's Restorative Love

Evangelism is most effective at the point where God's gospel purposes collide with our deepest human longings. What motivates people to respond to the actual gospel—not its parody that involves only trusting a savior, but the real gospel of King Jesus?

God's restorative love.

The condition into which we are all born—to be human—is to prefer to be king over our own lives rather than to submit to God's rule, leading to dishonor for ourselves, creation, and God. Attraction to King Jesus must overcome this repugnant desire for self-rule and its damaging consequences. God's restorative love heightens the attraction.

Even if non-Christians can't glimpse it yet, nonetheless God's love motivates. In love God creates a good world full of beauty and truth. God calls humans very good and gives them a special role as image-bearers. In the midst of our loathsome choices that have fractured our honor as image-bearers and harmed creation, God hates sin but doesn't hate us. On the contrary, he shows unfathomable new depths of his love by suffering on the cross for us. On the cross God reveals his pouring-out-the-self-for-the-sake-of-others character most fully.

God is emphatically for you and for me. We do not deserve the grace of the gospel. But God's love didn't stop with the gift of the cross and resurrection. He loves us so much that he graced us with a King who will live and reign forever, inviting us to be transformed by submitting to his kingship. Then we can become glorious rulers too, like Jesus. God's love launches us toward him, so that we can respond to Jesus's kingship.

Beauty, Goodness, and Truth

Hence, a winning strategy is to gospel backward to awaken an awareness of God's love. Even for those who don't believe God exists, we can start with *beauty, goodness, and truth.* This works because creation reveals God's invisible qualities to everyone, even to those who reject him (Rom. 1:19–20). Humans are bankrupt in reasoning and darkened in understanding so that we can't be saved apart from the grace of Jesus the Christ (Rom. 1:21, 28; 3:23–24). But once the gracious gift of the King has been given—and now it has—then Jesus and Paul both say that the light attracts *even those who are nonbelievers* (see discussion in chapter 6). As when a match brightens the darkness, non-Christians are aided when Christians help heighten their appreciation of beauty, goodness, and truth.

Personalizing Restoration

Leading with beauty, goodness, and truth makes sense because they are available universally. But that isn't their only advantage. They are especially effective because they resonate with the gospel's restorative purpose. *A heightened sense of original beauty sharpens awareness of present decay and amplifies a longing for recovery.*

We are most motivated to respond to the gospel when we detect *something good yet damaged*—something that we come to hope that allegiance to King Jesus can return to glory. For this reason, Christians should be quick to point out tarnished splendor.

The *something good yet damaged* that needs restoration will vary for each person. It may be *social*—fleeting experiences of true friendship amid the overall experience of isolation or hurt in relationships. It may be *aesthetic*—the beauty of creation before it was ravaged. It may be *theological*—an unshakeable awareness of God's goodness despite hearing people mock him. It might be *intellectual*—the elegant truths of physics amid the world's chaos. Most often it is *personal*—the sense that I truly am an honorable person, or at least that I could be one if I could just get out from under the weight of my shameful moral failings and harmful choices.

Complicit in Tarnishing

When sharing the gospel, Christians should be eager to add their personal testimony. But we need to testify backward too. Once an awareness of beauty, goodness, and truth has been awakened—and a longing to restore something specific—nonbelievers need to see that we *all* contribute to the brokenness. The best way for you to tell a nonbeliever about their complicity in brokenness is by telling stories about your own.

Don't lead with the victories you are experiencing under King Jesus. Speak vulnerably about the harms you've caused in the past— and the hurts still unfolding. Tell about your grudge toward your boss. Share how your father wounded your pride—and how you've struggled to forgive him. Announce your attraction to porn. Tell about how you let personal goals crush a friendship. In other words, share how your misguided choices have hurt others and creation, and how they have brought dishonor to God.

When you tell a non-Christian about the brokenness you've created, not only will they find your authenticity refreshing, but it will also indirectly help them weigh how they have caused similar damage so they can conclude that they need rescue too. When they see your brokenness, their own will be mirrored and amplified as they sympathize.

Detecting Glory through King Jesus

Lead with struggle and defeat but clearly announce King Jesus and his victories. We—insiders and outsiders alike—choose King Jesus when we're convinced that our self-rule is part of the problem and that allegiance to him can repair something valuable. With the Spirit's help, we remain Christian by persisting in this choice. In other words, we repent and express fidelity.

Again, personal testimony is key. Tell how allegiance to King Jesus is transforming you and your community so that dignity is being restored. Explain how Jesus's cross-shaped example helped you serve your boss so that your attitude about work is beginning to change. Detail how you were finally able to forgive your sister. Tell how your small group called you out for false self-shaming and helped you find esteem because of who you are becoming in the King. Share about the victory you experienced over sexual temptation for a season.

When personally testifying to Jesus's victories, announce that things still aren't perfect. Authenticity matters. Be truthful about where you are still shamefully struggling. Remind yourself and others: when I die to myself for my King, I truly find abundant life; but it is never complete, comfortable, or easy. Stress that allegiance brings real healing, but that it is a gradual and difficult battle. Sometimes you lose your footing. But loyalty to King Jesus keeps you struggling to move upward.

Allegiance for Glory's Restoration

Outsiders and insiders to Christianity are motivated to respond to the gospel most fully when they detect that restoration is truly happening around and through King Jesus. Because each of us is created to carry God's fame to creation, our desire for restoration of glory for ourselves, culture, creation, and God can be aroused by God's gift of King Jesus. So, in faith and hope, we attach ourselves to King Jesus, the vibrantly living one.

Let's share the good news with purpose. Out of his boundless love God gave the gospel. King Jesus alone is capable of restoring our God-given honor so we can carry it locally to creation. But King Jesus does more than restore. He enhances our reputation and creation's. Since God is its source, this enhanced honor redounds to God's ultimate glory.

Why the gospel? Because of his *love* for all creation, God is *rescuing* it through the gracious gift of a *King*. *Allegiance* to King Jesus results in *life* now and forevermore. When *transformed* humans forever *reign gloriously* with the King, then creation, humans, and above all God are appropriately *honored* as God intended.

Let's praise King Jesus, the glory restorer, now and forever!

Questions for Discussion or Reflection

1. This chapter opened with a story of evangelism gone wrong. What is the most cringeworthy example of evangelism that you've experienced? What would have been a better way to share the gospel in that specific circumstance?
2. Reread the "inadequate" versus the "better" gospel invitations. To help you (or your group) internalize the differences, try to explain how each handles content, decision point, individualization, and the gospel's purposes differently. How can you take practical steps from these toward a better gospel presentation?
3. Do you agree that personal plight is usually *not* the best starting point in sharing the gospel today? Why or why not?
4. How might heightening appreciation for truth, beauty, and

goodness in the world enhance evangelism? Think of three or four things you (or your group) can do locally this month to heighten appreciation for these things.

5. Think of two or three different examples of sinful behavior that frequently occur today. How does the harm done bring dishonor on humans, creation, and God? When restoration to full honor is achieved with and under King Jesus, what is the process and final result in each case?

6. What are some ways in which you are complicit in harm and brokenness? How is King Jesus bringing restoration? In what areas of your life is recovery still most urgently needed? How can your story of brokenness become a gospel opportunity?

7. Think of three people who you think need to hear or re-hear the gospel. What is *something good yet damaged* that each would readily recognize and appreciate? Imagine what shape a conversation about King Jesus might take with each. Commit to praying for each.

8. In the end, *why the gospel*? That is, why did God give the gospel? And why is the gospel still the best possible news today?

Recommended Resources

In making recommendations, I've restricted the list primarily to the field of New Testament studies, with an eye toward recent books that are especially important for understanding the gospel, faith, grace, image, glory, and salvation.

Introductory

Matthew W. Bates. *Gospel Allegiance*. Grand Rapids: Brazos, 2019.
Matthew W. Bates. *The Gospel Precisely*. Nashville: Renew.org, 2021.
Michael Bird. *Introducing Paul*. Downers Grove: IVP Academic, 2009.
Carmen Joy Imes. *Bearing God's Name*. Downers Grove: IVP Academic, 2019.
Scot McKnight. *The King Jesus Gospel*. Grand Rapids: Zondervan, 2011.
N. T. Wright. *How God Became King*. New York: HarperOne, 2012.
N. T. Wright. *Simply Good News*. New York: HarperOne, 2015.

Intermediate

Matthew W. Bates. *Salvation by Allegiance Alone*. Grand Rapids: Baker Academic, 2017.
Michael J. Gorman. *Becoming the Gospel*. Grand Rapids: Eerdmans, 2015.

Michael J. Gorman. *Romans*. Grand Rapids: Eerdmans, 2022.

Kenneth Keathley. *Salvation and Sovereignty*. Nashville: B&H Academic, 2010.

Patrick Schreiner. *The Ascension of Christ*. Bellingham, WA: Lexham, 2020.

Alan R. Streett. *Caesar and the Sacrament*. Eugene, OR: Cascade, 2018.

N. T. Wright. *The Challenge of Jesus*. Downers Grove: IVP, 1999.

Advanced

John Barclay. *Paul and the Gift*. Grand Rapids: Eerdmans, 2015.

Nijay Gupta. *Paul and the Language of Faith*. Grand Rapids: Eerdmans, 2020.

Haley Goranson Jacob. *Conformed to the Image of His Son*. Downers Grove: IVP Academic, 2018.

Joshua W. Jipp. *Christ Is King*. Minneapolis: Fortress, 2015.

Joshua W. Jipp. *The Messianic Theology of the New Testament*. Grand Rapids: Eerdmans, 2019.

Scot McKnight. *Reading Romans Backwards*. Waco, TX: Baylor University Press, 2019.

Teresa Morgan. *Roman Faith and Christian Faith*. Oxford: Oxford University Press, 2015.

Enoch O. Okode. *Christ the Gift and the Giver*. Eugene, OR: Cascade, 2022.

Jonathan T. Pennington. *The Sermon on the Mount and Human Flourishing*. Grand Rapids: Baker Academic, 2017.

Paul A. Rainbow. *The Way of Salvation*. Milton Keynes: Paternoster, 2005.

Julian C. H. Smith. *Paul and the Good Life*. Waco, TX: Baylor University Press.

N. T. Wright. *Jesus and the Victory of God*. Minneapolis: Fortress, 1996.

N. T. Wright. *Paul and the Faithfulness of God*. 2 Volumes. Minneapolis: Fortress, 2013.

Jackson Wu. *Reading Romans with Eastern Eyes*. Downers Grove: IVP Academic, 2019.

Notes

Chapter 1

1. 1QS 9:11 in *The Dead Sea Scrolls: A New Translation*, trans. Michael Wise, Martin Abegg Jr., and Edward Cook, rev. ed. (San Francisco: HarperSanFrancisco: 2005), 131.

2. See Josephus, *War* 2.433–34; 2.56; 2.652–53; 4.507–13; 7.29–31; and *Antiquities* 17.271–85; 20.97–98.

3. Josephus, *Antiquities* 18.109–119.

4. 4Q521 Frags 2 + 4 Col. 2 in *The Dead Sea Scrolls*, 531.

5. N. T. Wright, *Simply Good News: Why the Gospel Is News and What Makes It Good* (New York: HarperOne, 2011), 13.

6. For this paragraph I draw especially upon my earlier articulation in Matthew W. Bates, *Gospel Allegiance: What Faith in Jesus Misses for Salvation in Christ* (Grand Rapids: Brazos, 2019), 42–43.

7. For a summary and links to the prior discussion, see Matthew W. Bates, "Why T4G/TGC Leaders Must Fix Their Gospel," *Christianity Today Blog Forum*, April 29, 2020, https://www.christianitytoday.com/scot-mcknight/2020/april/why-t4gtgc-leaders-must-fix-their-gospel.html.

8. John Barclay, *Paul and the Gift* (Grand Rapids: Eerdmans, 2015); and David DeSilva, *Patronage, Honor, Kinship, and Purity: Unlocking New Testament Culture* (Downers Grove, IL: InterVarsity, 2000), 95–120.

9. Teresa Morgan, *Roman Faith and Christian Faith: Pistis and Fides in the Early Roman Empire and Early Churches* (Oxford: Oxford University Press, 2015), 14, 23, 503; for recent scholarship, see Matthew W. Bates, "The External-Relational Shift in Faith (*Pistis*) in New Testament Research: Romans 1 as a Gospel-Allegiance Test Case," *Currents in Biblical Research* 18 (2020): 176–202.

10. Nijay Gupta, *Paul and the Language of Faith* (Grand Rapids: Eerdmans, 2020), 13.

Chapter 2

1. Lyrics by Adam Duritz, "Mr. Jones," from Counting Crows album *August and Everything After*, Geffen Records, 1993.

2. See Matthew W. Bates, *Gospel Allegiance* (Grand Rapids: Brazos, 2019), for an attempt to articulate the true relationship among the gospel, faith, grace, works, righteousness, and eternal life.

3. Scot McKnight, *The King Jesus Gospel: The Original Good News Revisited* (Grand Rapids: Zondervan, 2011).

4. BDAG, s.v. *doxa*, p. 257.

5. See 1 Clement 5.5–7, the text of which can be found in Rick Brannan, *The Apostolic Fathers: A New Translation* (Bellingham, WA: Lexham, 2017), 15.

6. Lyric changes per the album, *Across the Live Wire*, accessed June 1, 2022, https://open.spotify.com/album/1tqB9q7YnXgWekLtO6wggy.

7. Adam Duritz, "'It Takes Its Toll,'" interview by Dan Cain, *The Sun*, September 16, 2018, https://www.thesun.co.uk/tvandshowbiz/7252075/counting-crows-adam-duritz-famous-musicians/.

Chapter 3

1. C. S. Lewis, *The Great Divorce* (New York: Touchstone, 1996), 105.

2. Lewis, *The Great Divorce*, 106.

3. Lewis, *The Great Divorce*, 106–7.

4. Here the NIV translates "heavenly beings," but more precisely the original Hebrew reads "sons of God," a designation elsewhere for angels (e.g., Job 1:6; 2:1).

5. Jackson Wu, *Reading Romans with Eastern Eyes: Honor and Shame in Paul's Message and Mission* (Downers Grove, IL: IVP Academic, 2019), 43. Italics original to the quote.

6. Greg K. Beale, *We Become What We Worship: A Biblical Theology of Idolatry* (Downers Grove, IL: IVP Academic, 2008).

Chapter 4

1. Matthew W. Bates, *Gospel Allegiance: What Faith in Jesus Misses for Salvation in Christ* (Grand Rapids: Brazos, 2019), 86–87; and Matthew W. Bates, *The Gospel Precisely: Surprisingly Good News about Jesus Christ the King* (Nashville: Renew.org, 2021), 34.

2. Carmen Joy Imes, introduction to *Bearing God's Name: Why Sinai Still Matters* (Downers Grove, IL: IVP Academic, 2019).

3. Joshua M. McNall, *The Mosaic of Atonement: An Integrated Approach to Christ's Work* (Grand Rapids: Zondervan Academic, 2019).

4. For example, as in Isa. 45:13 LXX; and Josephus, *Antiquities* 12.28, 33, 46; 14.107, 371; *War* 1.274, 384.

5. Origen, *Commentary on Romans* 2.13.29, trans. Thomas P. Scheck, *Origen: Commentary on the Epistle to the Romans*, The Fathers of the Church (Washington, DC: Catholic University of America Press, 2001), 1:161.

6. Cyprian, Epistle 59, trans. Ernest Wallis, in *The Ante-Nicene Fathers*, ed. Alexander Roberts and James Donaldson (1886; repr., Peabody, MA: Hendrickson, 2004), 5:355.

7. Patrick Schreiner, *The Ascension of the Christ: Recovering a Neglected Doctrine* (Bellingham, WA: Lexham, 2020), 115.

8. For a brief but thoughtful article, see David Moffitt, "What's Up with the Ascension?," *Christianity Today*, May 21, 2020, https://www.christianitytoday.com/ct/2020/may-web-only/whats-up-with-ascension.html.

Chapter 5

1. Roald Dahl, *Charlie and the Chocolate Factory* (New York: Puffin, 2007), 33–34. Italics original to the quote.

2. Dahl, *Charlie and the Chocolate Factory*, 129–35, with the quotes appearing on 130 and 134.

3. Shel Silverstein, *Where the Sidewalk Ends* (New York: HarperCollins Children's Books, 1996), 28–29.

4. James K. A. Smith, *You Are What You Love: The Spiritual Power of Habit* (Grand Rapids: Brazos, 2016).

5. See Matthew W. Bates, *The Birth of the Trinity: Jesus, God, and Spirit in New Testament and Early Christian Interpretations of the Old Testament* (Oxford: Oxford University Press, 2015).

6. Jonathan T. Pennington, *The Sermon on the Mount and Human Flourishing: A Theological Commentary* (Grand Rapids: Baker Academic, 2017), 14.

7. Joshua W. Jipp, *Christ Is King: Paul's Royal Ideology* (Minneapolis: Fortress, 2015), 45.

8. Charles Wesley, "Christ the Lord Is Risen Today," 1739.

9. Graham Kendrick, "Shine Jesus Shine," Make Way Music, 1987.

Chapter 6

1. Joshua Harris, "My Heart Is Full of Gratitude," Instagram post, July 26, 2019, https://www.instagram.com/p/B0ZBrNLH2sl/.

2. Barna Group data cited in David Kinnaman and Gabe Lyons, *UnChristian:*

What a New Generation Really Thinks about Christianity . . . and Why It Matters (Grand Rapids: Baker Books, 2007), 29–30.

3. Kinnaman and Lyons, *UnChristian*, 166.

4. Kinnaman and Lyons, *UnChristian*, 156.

5. David Kinnaman, *You Lost Me: Why Young Christians Are Leaving Church . . . and Rethinking Faith* (Grand Rapids: Baker Books, 2011).

6. Kinnaman, *You Lost Me*, 28–30.

7. See Matthew W. Bates, *Salvation by Allegiance Alone: Rethinking Faith, Works, and the Gospel of Jesus the King* (Grand Rapids: Baker Academic, 2017); Matthew W. Bates, *Gospel Allegiance: What Faith in Jesus Misses for Salvation in Christ* (Grand Rapids: Brazos, 2019); Scot McKnight, *Reading Romans Backwards: A Gospel of Peace in the Midst of Empire* (Waco, Texas: Baylor University Press, 2019); and Michael J. Gorman, *Romans: A Pastoral and Theological Commentary* (Grand Rapids: Eerdmans, 2022).

8. This analysis of the thief draws on my earlier work. See Bates, *Gospel Allegiance*, 108–9.

9. Dallas Willard, *The Great Omission: Reclaiming Jesus's Essential Teachings on Discipleship* (New York: HarperOne, 2006), 14.

10. Kinnaman, *You Lost Me*, 44–50.

11. Kinnaman, *You Lost Me*, 205.

12. Bobby Harrington and Josh Patrick, *The Disciple Maker's Handbook: Seven Elements of a Discipleship Lifestyle* (Grand Rapids: Zondervan, 2017).

13. Mitch's story is reported by John Marriott, *The Anatomy of Deconversion: Keys to a Lifelong Faith in a Culture Abandoning Christianity* (Abilene, TX: Abilene Christian University Press, 2021), 66.

14. Dennis R. Venema and Scot McKnight, *Adam and the Genome: Reading Scripture after Genetic Science* (Grand Rapids: Brazos, 2017).

15. See Bates, *Gospel Allegiance*, esp. 107–8, 177–210.

16. Eugene's story is told by Kinnaman, *You Lost Me*, 82

17. Benjamin's story is told by Marriott, *Anatomy of Deconversion*, 232–33.

Chapter 7

1. I am describing the typical New Testament process, but famously there are exceptions. For example, the gift of the Holy Spirit is temporarily withheld from those who are baptized when the gospel is accepted in Samaria (Acts 8:14–17) and it comes before water baptism when the gentiles first enter the church (Acts 10:44–48). These extraordinary cases show that God is orchestrating the expansion of the gospel's saving reach as it moves from Jerusalem to Samaria and then to all nations.

2. R. Alan Streett, *Caesar and the Sacrament: Baptism: A Rite of Resistance* (Eugene, OR: Cascade, 2018), 105.

INDEX OF SUBJECTS

INDEX OF SCRIPTURE
AND OTHER ANCIENT WRITINGS